THE
BABY SLEEP
GUIDE

Practical Advice to
Establish Good Sleep Habits

THE BABY SLEEP GUIDE

An Hachette UK Company
www.hachette.co.uk

Vie Books, an imprint of Summersdale Publishers Ltd
Part of Octopus Publishing Group Limited
Carmelite House
50 Victoria Embankment
LONDON
EC4Y 0DZ
UK

www.summersdale.com

Printed and bound by CPI Group (UK) Ltd, Croydon, CR0 4YY

ISBN: 978-1-84953-685-1

P. 23 SIDS information has been reproduced with kind permission of The Lullaby Trust.

Substantial discounts on bulk quantities of Summersdale books are available to corporations, professional associations and other organisations. For details contact general enquiries: telephone: +44 (0) 1243 771107 or email: enquiries@summersdale.com.

Disclaimer
The information given in this book should not be treated as a substitute for qualified medical advice. Neither the author nor the publisher can be held responsible for any loss or claim arising out of the use, or misuse, of the suggestions made or the failure to take medical advice.
The case studies and quotes included in this book are based on the real experiences of individuals and families, however, in some cases, names have been changed to protect privacy.

THE
BABY SLEEP
GUIDE

Practical Advice to
Establish Good Sleep Habits

Stephanie Modell

Inspired by my children:
Alexander, Evangeline and Maxwell

Contents

Part Six: Further Resources and Information.....131

FOREWORD

By Jill Irving

RN (adult) RN (child) RM RHV JP

Over 30 years ago when I became a health visitor, I thought lack of sleep was what happened after a late night out with friends. I had little concept what any parent with a young sleepless child may be enduring until I became a parent myself.

My first son was born during the mid 1980s, and I had been a health visitor for eight years by the time his non-sleeping brother arrived. I was meant to be supporting parents who were struggling with their own sleep-challenged babies, but I found it difficult to cope with even the simplest daily tasks in my own life.

For many years the only professional sleep advice recommended was controlled crying, or for those that were desperate, medication. Yes, for many years health professionals were recommending prescribed medication for children as young as six months old!

As hard as it may seem, it has only been since we've reached the twenty-first century that sleep problems amongst babies and young children have been acknowledged to be an increasing and serious problem.

Before this, parents were led to believe that it was normal for their babies and young children to regularly take hours to settle and spend hours awake each night. Parents were expected to get on with it as best they could, with virtually little or no support.

In a major online sleep survey by Mumsnet of parents with children aged 0–10 years in July 2012, 11,000 mothers said that more than half had children waking at night; nearly a quarter of parents said their relationship had suffered; and almost a third said they felt regularly sleep deprived and exhausted. Without doubt this is a serious issue.

Research has also told us that directly or indirectly, lack of sleep can affect families by increasing the risk of postnatal depression, domestic violence and harm to children, separation and divorce rates, road traffic accidents, and affect work performance.

Thankfully, sleep consultants like Stephanie Modell are beginning to change parents' lives. Even better, Stephanie has produced this wonderfully simple-to-follow evidence-based guide for all those involved with babies and young children. Even if you are tired and exhausted, Stephanie gently leads you through each stage so that you gradually feel you are taking back some control of your life.

If you are expecting your first baby, buy this book now. If you are a parent struggling with a night-owl, buy this book now. If you are an excited grandparent to be, or just about to go to a girlfriend's or relative's baby shower, ditch the cute booties and buy this book instead. This will be the best gift you could buy any potential parent.

Every health professional working with babies and young children should have at least two copies of this book in their office, as once they've lent out the first copy they'll never get it back!

Jill Irving
January 2015

Jill Irving has been a practising health visitor for 33 years. She is the health visiting expert for babycentre.co.uk.

Introduction

There are hundreds of sleep books available but many contradict each other, they are long and wordy and can make sleep a very complicated subject. My aim is to offer something different. I want you to find out for yourself that sleep is not a difficult subject and that you will be able to achieve a good night's sleep for both you and your baby if you can put good practices in place early on. I want you to discover that a well-rested baby is a contented baby. I'm not going to promise you that I can get your baby to sleep for 12 hours a night at 12 weeks old. Babies do wake at night, but you can help them to learn to sleep with some gentle guidance, by following their own body rhythms and encouraging them to self-settle. Babies are only capable of learning what we teach them. Helping your baby to discover his own way of settling is a fundamental step in encouraging him to sleep through the night. By establishing positive sleep habits early on, controlled crying should NEVER be necessary!

It's hard to absorb everything you are told and all that you read, particularly when you are tired and hormonal, so my intention is not to give you an exhaustive book about sleep but one that provides you with the essential information. Knowledge is empowering. I really do believe that if you understand the basic biology of sleep, you are much less likely to experience sleep problems with your baby. As a mother of 17-year-old triplets, my advice is not only gleaned from professional experience but also first-hand when teaching my own children to sleep through the night.

When you are pregnant you receive mounds of information about what to expect with regard to the actual birth and what will follow but the feedback I receive from parents is that postnatal information regarding sleep is lacking. The aim of this book is to fill that gap, with easy-to-read, accessible information on what is sometimes perceived to be the most difficult part of being a parent.

If possible, I highly recommend that you read this during pregnancy and again in the early weeks.

I have chosen to refer to your baby as 'he' throughout the book, to avoid sounding impersonal, however, clearly, my advice is for all babies, male and female.

If I could only say one thing!

If I could only say one thing to new parents it would be: 'Do not teach your baby to fall asleep while feeding.' In fact, I wouldn't just say this, I would shout it from the rooftops!

Don't get me wrong, feeding a baby to sleep and for comfort is fine and positively encouraged in those first precious weeks while you are bonding with your baby and establishing your milk supply if you choose to breastfeed. A newborn's sucking reflex is strong and allowing him to satisfy his sucking needs at this time will help you to establish an adequate and stable milk supply. Breast milk also contains a range of hormones which have a soporific effect on babies and will induce sleep, especially during the early weeks when your baby sleeps in short but regular sleep cycles for optimal development.

However, the most common problem I come across as a sleep consultant is babies who have never learnt to fall asleep without a breast or bottle in their mouths, which in turn causes frequent night-time waking.

If your baby can only get himself to sleep in this way, he will be unable to self-settle and will be totally dependent on feeding to sleep. Is this fair on him? As he gets older he will not have the ability to return to sleep at points during the night-time sleep cycle where he naturally wakes. This will result in frequent waking and he will always need to be nursed or fed back to sleep again.

The kindest thing you can do for your baby is to teach him to self-settle while he is very young by introducing alternative sleep cues. If you were always to tie your child's shoelaces for him, he would never learn to do so himself. The same goes for sleep, if you always feed a baby to sleep he will never be able to settle himself to sleep independently or 'self-soothe' as it's sometimes known.

> **The kindest thing you can do for your baby is to teach him to self-settle while he is very young.**

Having experienced sleep problems with my first child who I ended up cuddling or feeding to sleep at all times, I was determined to teach my second baby to settle independently. Within just a few weeks, I could put Savanna down in her cot and she would literally just go to sleep!

Angela, mother of Savanna, now aged 12 months.

Parenting styles

I work with families who have a variety of different parenting styles and I adapt sleep solutions to suit each family. It is really important that you use sleep techniques that you feel comfortable with.

There are a number of publications covering two conflicting methods of parenting. One being the development of a routine with a sometimes rigid feed and sleep schedule, as encouraged by Gina Ford in The Complete Sleep Guide for Contented Babies. The second being 'close proximity or attachment parenting' as described by William and Martha Sears in The Attachment Parenting Book, whereby parents and baby co-sleep in the parental bed and the baby is encouraged to feed as and when they wish and is carried in a sling throughout the day, often referred to as 'baby wearing'.

As parents, of course you want a securely attached child, and to achieve this you need to nurture a strong parent–child connection by meeting their physical, mental and emotional needs. Therefore if you choose to parent in a more traditional Western style, as long as you meet your baby's natural needs you are no less 'attached' to your baby so this term should not be misinterpreted. The most important points to consider if you choose to co-sleep are the safety implications.

You should never co-sleep if you or your partner is a smoker, has consumed alcohol or drugs or if either of you is excessively tired. There are also increased risks if your baby was born prematurely or had a low birth weight. Guidance on co-sleeping safely can be found at www.lullabytrust.org.uk and www.nct.org.uk. I would also strongly advise that you teach your baby to sleep independently in his cot or Moses basket for some daytime naps. Once your baby is 8–9 months old and on the move it can prove to be a real problem if he can only fall asleep when co-sleeping with you in the parental bed. You may end up having to go to bed at 8 p.m. with your baby in order to get him to sleep and you may have to lay down with him for naps if he does not know how to go to sleep in any other way.

I have worked with many families that have ended up co-sleeping because they have been unable to get their baby to sleep in any other way. In this type of instance, it is not a planned lifestyle choice but 'accidental parenting' or 'reactive co-sleeping', which can cause resentment.

With regard to parenting to a strict clock based schedule, this may work for some babies but all babies are unique so one schedule cannot work for all babies and parents. Within the realms of 'average sleep needs' and 'average sleep cycles' there can, of course, be a great disparity. A baby's feed requirements will also differ depending on how they feed, their ability to feed efficiently, their health and tolerance to their milk feeds. If a mother is breastfeeding, her milk production will play a factor in how often her baby needs to feed. For so many reasons, including our wonderful uniqueness, prescriptive clock based parenting cannot work for all.

Parenting today can seem wildly polarised: breast versus bottle; purees versus baby-led weaning; routine versus attachment, whereas most mums in real life find a healthy balance between the two. I encourage you to go with the flow in those first few precious weeks while you recover from the huge journey of birth, getting to know your baby and establishing feeding, whether it be breast or bottle. I then aim to bridge opposing attitudes by advocating a blend of common sense, gentle guidance, practical advice and a lot of love.

I don't believe that you need to make a choice as to whether to follow 'attachment' parenting or a structured style of parenting. There is a middle road, where you can have the best of both by following your baby's rhythms and cues to connect the bridge between nurture and structure by encouraging some sleep independence and adopting a flexible routine.

Part One:
SLEEP - THE BASICS

1. Safe sleep

Babies need a lot of sleep during the first few months of their lives so it's important to ensure that they are sleeping as safely as possible.

Sudden infant death syndrome (SIDS) is the sudden and unexplained death of a baby where no cause is found. While SIDS is rare, it can still happen and there are steps that parents can take to help reduce the chance of this tragedy occurring.

The Lullaby Trust is a British charitable organisation, considered the recognised national authority on safe sleeping practices for infants and children. They recommend that parents follow their advice (below) to significantly reduce the risk of SIDS. Aim to follow the advice for all sleep periods, not just at night.

Things you can do

★ **Always place your baby on their back to sleep, with their feet positioned at the bottom of the cot.**

★ **Keep your baby smoke free during pregnancy and after birth.**

★ **Place your baby to sleep in a separate cot or Moses basket in the same room as you for the first 6 months.**

★ **Breastfeed your baby, if you can.**

★ **Use a firm, flat, waterproof mattress in good condition.**

Things to avoid

★ **Never sleep on a sofa or in an armchair with your baby.**

★ **Don't sleep in the same bed as your baby if you smoke, drink or take drugs or are extremely tired, if your baby was born prematurely or was of low birth-weight.**

★ **Avoid letting your baby get too hot.**

★ **Don't cover your baby's face or head while sleeping or use loose bedding or pillows.**

More information can be found at www.lullabytrust.org.uk.

2. Medical conditions

There are a lot of books on medical conditions, so I will keep this section brief. The most likely problems you may face with an otherwise healthy baby are colic, reflux and milk/lactose intolerance. These can be difficult to diagnose, but if your baby is terribly unhappy day in, day out, is very difficult to settle and seems to be crying in pain, seek medical help. Trust your instincts.

Your baby will be difficult to settle if he experiences any of the above so you will need to do a lot more cuddling, rocking and soothing. If you are following medical advice, you may also not be able to space your feeds as I have suggested. In any of these situations, just give your baby the attention he needs, I know it's terribly hard and you will be exhausted but your baby's condition will improve with time and help. Try to sleep when your baby sleeps and accept any offers of help. Above all, try not to cope alone.

Babies who experience colic usually start to improve around 3 months old, while with severe reflux, unfortunately it can take longer. I suggest you do whatever you can to help your baby to settle but as soon as he is ready and the situation begins to improve, teach him to self-settle using the gradual retreat process, explained in sections 15 and 20. He will be much happier for it. Sleep is a great healer.

3. Why is sleep important?

Sleep is essential for the physical and psychological health of your child. Studies have proved that a good night's sleep and regular bedtime routine have a significantly positive impact on a child's well-being, particularly their behaviour and ability to learn. Lack of sleep has been linked with obesity, aggression, behaviour problems, low IQ and poor memory.

Sleep deprivation has a negative impact on the whole family. Sleep deprived parents are likely to find parenting challenging, and a lack of sleep can have much wider-ranging consequences including a negative effect on parents' relationships with each other and their children.

Sleep problems are common and preventable. Although I will stress the importance of establishing positive sleep habits early on, it's never too late to help your child and furthermore, studies have shown that children who have good sleep habits are less likely to experience sleep problems such as insomnia in adult life. When you help your child to learn to sleep well, you often see a dramatic improvement in their mood, appetite and behaviour.

> **A good night's sleep has a significant impact on a child's health, well-being, behaviour and ability to learn.**

We embarked on a programme of 'sleep teaching' when my son was 13 months old. Up until then, we had both had very little sleep. It wasn't easy as I had fallen into negative habits that had to be undone. However, after a couple of months, my son's nursery teacher said that she couldn't believe the change in him, he was so much more content and his appetite had improved also.

Anna, mother of Thomas, aged 16 months.

Average sleep needs chart

This chart shows the 'average' sleep needs of a baby or child, but please bear in mind the 'average' can vary greatly between babies, so only refer to this as a guide.

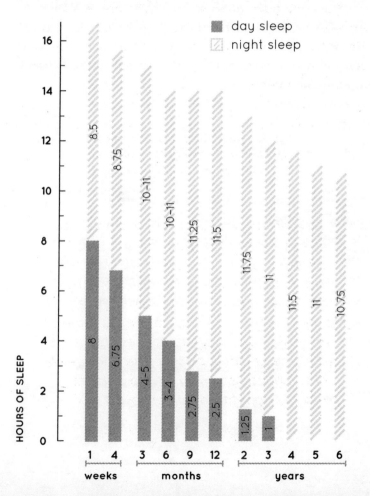

Legend:
- day sleep
- night sleep

Night sleep values: 8.5, 8.75, 10-11, 10-11, 11.25, 11.5, 11.75, 11, 11.5, 11, 10.75

Day sleep values: 8, 6.75, 4-5, 3-4, 2.75, 2.5, 1.25, 1

Y-axis: HOURS OF SLEEP (0, 2, 4, 6, 8, 10, 12, 14, 16)

X-axis: 1, 4 (weeks); 3, 6, 9, 12 (months); 2, 3, 4, 5, 6 (years)

4. Understanding sleep

Types of sleep

When we go to sleep it's not a simple matter of switching off and waking up in the morning, we go through cycles, experiencing various stages along the way from drowsiness to light sleep, through to deep sleep. Even though your body is resting and restoring its energy levels, sleep is an active state, essential for your physical and mental well-being. We can divide sleep into two broad types:

Non-REM sleep (non-rapid eye movement sleep)

Non-REM sleep is a deep sleep where the brain rests; blood is released to the muscles; tissue is grown or repaired; hormones are released for growth and development; and white blood cells are made to support the immune system. During non-REM sleep your baby will breathe steadily and deeply and will be hard to wake.

> **Non-REM sleep is not fully developed until your baby is around 4 months old.**

REM sleep (rapid eye movement sleep)

REM sleep is vital to the development of the brain and it is the state in which we dream. The body rests, extra blood is released to the brain and the baby processes what he has seen and heard during the day. Young babies spend a lot of time in REM sleep due to its developmental importance.

REM sleep is sometimes known as 'dream sleep'.

It is essential that we teach our babies and children to sleep through the night, so they can achieve a sufficient amount of both types of sleep to aid their development.

Sleep hormones

There are two key hormones connected with sleep and it helps to understand the importance of each.

Melatonin

Also known as the sleep hormone, melatonin regulates sleep by telling your body it's night-time and it's time to go to bed. When your baby goes to sleep at night, it's beneficial for melatonin levels to be high. You can help to influence this by having a good predictable bed and bath time routine. Melatonin is produced primarily in darkness so keep the lights low and avoid any exposure to TV or computer screens close to bedtime as the blue lights emitted from such devices inhibit the production of melatonin. A baby's melatonin levels increase around the age of 3 months, so this is your real window of opportunity to establish a routine and teach your baby to sleep. However, if you miss this window, don't feel disheartened as it is never too late to establish a routine.

> **Melatonin levels increase at around 3 months of age, so this is your real window of opportunity to establish a routine and teach your baby to sleep.**

Cortisol

This is the hormone created when the body is overtired and sleep deprived. It's sometimes known as the stress hormone. If your baby's cortisol levels are high, he will find it very difficult to go to sleep, which is why you need to encourage good daytime naps. Too much cortisol can also cause regular night-time waking and early rising.

You can often see the effect of cortisol in older children who are not good sleepers, they appear to be active, 'wired' and on the go all the time. Parents may think they have a child who needs less sleep than their peers as they are full of energy, but actually their body is releasing cortisol as a way to cope with their fatigue. This is not healthy, the child needs more sleep!

Too much cortisol is like a dose of caffeine!

5. Sleep cycles

Just as you sleep in cycles, so does your baby. When he is newborn these sleep cycles are short, however, by the age of around 3–4 months your baby's sleep cycles will begin to lengthen and he will start to establish the sleep cycle pattern that he will maintain for life. During daytime naps these sleep cycles are approximately 45 minutes, however, at night these will start to extend to approximately 90 minutes.

Given the fact that sleep cycles extend and melatonin levels increase from around 3 months of age your baby should be able to sleep for more extended periods at night by this time.

In addition, at this age, the circadian rhythm, better known as the body clock, is maturing. This is the 24-hour sequence of biological cycles which influence patterns of sleeping, waking, rest, hunger, activity, body temperature and hormones. This is why babies and children respond so well to routine to keep these rhythms in harmony.

This is the ideal time to guide your baby into a healthy routine, establish regular feed times, nap times, follow a predictable bath and bedtime routine and encourage self-settling.

This is a diagram to illustrate how a typical 6-month-plus baby goes through a roller coaster of sleep cycles throughout the night, transitioning through various stages of sleep, from drowsiness to light sleep, through to deep (non-REM) sleep and experiencing periods of dream (REM) sleep along the way.

The periods of brief waking throughout the night are nature's way of checking that our environment is safe. These brief wakings can become a problem if a child cannot settle themselves back to sleep alone and require the help of a parent or a feed to get themselves back to sleep again.

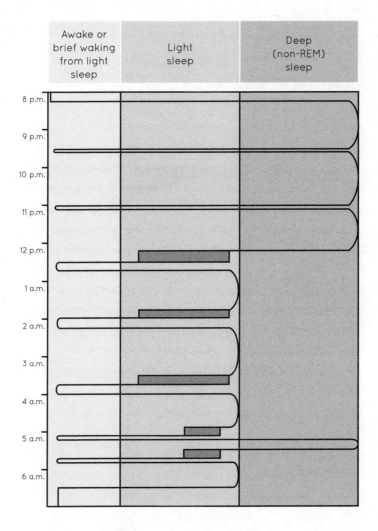

| Awake or brief waking from light sleep | Light sleep | Deep (non-REM) sleep |

8 p.m.
9 p.m.
10 p.m.
11 p.m.
12 p.m.
1 a.m.
2 a.m.
3 a.m.
4 a.m.
5 a.m.
6 a.m.

DREAM (REM) SLEEP

6. Understanding sleep cycles will help you to help your baby

From 3–4 months of age your baby will be rousing approximately every 60–90 minutes during the night. This is possibly the most important fact about your baby's sleep that you need to grasp. It is normal for babies to wake regularly during the night, this is nature's way of keeping us safe, but the key to prevent them from fully waking is for them to have the ability to settle themselves back to sleep again. Alongside the ability to self-settle your baby needs to find himself in exactly the same conditions when he rouses as when he fell asleep at the start of the night. Having the security that 'all is well' will give him the confidence to drift off again and only fully wake if he is hungry or has other needs.

  Here are some examples of scenarios to explain the importance of making your baby feel safe and secure:

 1. Your baby falls asleep in your arms, being cuddled or rocked. You move him to his cot while he is asleep. During the night he rouses, and instead of finding himself in the warm arms of a parent he is alone in his cot. He does not understand

how he has got there, and therefore wakes and cries so he can be rocked or cuddled to sleep again. This is equivalent to you falling asleep in your bed and waking up on the floor!

2. Your baby nurses to sleep or falls asleep while sucking on his bottle and then you put him in his cot. During the night, he rouses. He is unable to get back to sleep independently as he only knows how to get to sleep while sucking. He therefore wakes to be nursed or fed back to sleep.

3. Your baby falls asleep in his cot but with the musical mobile playing. There is noise and movement, maybe even a light show. When he rouses during the night it's silent and still. He is disturbed by the change in his conditions, so does not feel safe and secure, and therefore he cries for attention.

4. Your baby is put into his cot drowsy but awake. He falls asleep unaided in his cot, with no music or props. He may have a little cry. This is absolutely normal. It's rarely a cry of distress; your baby is helping himself get off to sleep. I think of this as letting off steam or releasing tension. When he rouses between sleep cycles during the night, he finds himself

in **exactly** the same conditions that he fell asleep in. He feels safe and secure, and he connects to his next sleep cycle unaided. He may have a moan, grizzle or cry while doing this which is quite normal. Don't be tempted to lift him unless he is distressed or due a feed.

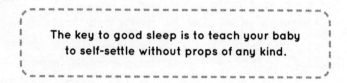

The key to good sleep is to teach your baby to self-settle without props of any kind.

Part Two:

TEACH YOUR BABY TO SLEEP

Babies can learn to fall asleep in response to external cues from their carer. Teaching your baby to self-settle when he is very young is generally not difficult. You can gently guide him by giving him the opportunity to learn to settle himself, or self-soothe. If you establish positive sleep habits early on, you will never need to try the dreaded controlled crying technique! However, if your baby cannot self-settle because he's learnt to be dependent on an inappropriate sleep association, for example, feeding or rocking to sleep, you will have to undo this habit in the future and this can be distressing.

A short-term fix can easily become a long-term habit.

7. Sleep associations

Helping your baby to discover his own way of self-settling is a fundamental step in encouraging him to sleep through the night. If your baby has fallen asleep dependent on any kind of prop, he will wake repeatedly during the night and need to be helped back to sleep again. Parents often tell me that their baby will only go to sleep while being rocked or fed. This is what their baby has been taught so they need to teach their baby to self-settle and thereby develop strategies to help him connect his sleep cycles independently during the night.

Inappropriate sleep associations or 'props'

★ **Feeding to sleep – breast or bottle**
★ **Rocking**
★ **Cuddling**
★ **Patting**
★ **Music**
★ **Motion – car/pushchair**
★ **Dummy**

> **Going to sleep is learnt behaviour. Your baby isn't born with sleep associations.**

Dummies

Whether or not you should use a dummy as a pacifier for your baby is a matter of constant debate. There seems to be little concrete evidence to suggest the benefit or harm in the long term, however, the Lullaby Trust's guidelines state that some research suggests it is possible that using a dummy when putting a baby down to sleep might reduce the risk of sudden infant death syndrome. It advises not to give a pacifier to a baby before the age of 4 weeks and, if you are breastfeeding, to wait until breastfeeding is well established, usually around 4-6 weeks. This should avoid your baby getting 'nipple confusion', which is the term used when a baby has difficulty latching onto the breast due to the early introduction of a dummy or a teat which involves using a different sucking technique to that of breast feeding. It advises to then stop using the dummy when your baby is 6-12 months old, however, in my opinion it can be quite difficult to remove a dummy at this stage as your baby will have learnt to go to sleep sucking so it will be a strong sleep association.

If a baby has learnt to fall asleep sucking a dummy this is likely to be the only way they can easily fall asleep. This can become a problem as, inevitably, the dummy parts company with baby during a sleep and when baby needs to suck on the dummy to connect to the next sleep cycle he is not physically able to find it and put it back into his mouth. Baby then cries and mum or dad has to come and pop the dummy back in. This can happen repeatedly during the night so it's something to be aware of if you choose to use one. To help an older baby to find their dummy during the night you can purchase small soft toys which the dummies easily attach to and these make it easier for baby to locate it independently in the night.

Ideally you will teach your baby to sleep without the aid of a prop but at the end of the day you are the only person who can judge what is right for your baby in your circumstances. Premature babies are often given dummies in hospital to help stimulate their suck before they are able to breast or bottle feed efficiently, and if you have a baby suffering from colic or reflux, sucking on a dummy can be a great source of comfort to them; just be aware not to use the dummy continually, try to only give it when necessary.

The human dummy

Has your baby finished breastfeeding? Gently unlatch him from the breast, wind him and then have some play and interaction time. If you allow him to continue to suckle he is using you for comfort rather than food, which is acceptable and positively encouraged in the early weeks, when he is getting used to this world, but it is unfair to teach him to become dependent on nursing as a sleep aid. When you are giving him his last feed before bedtime, try not to allow him to fall asleep on the breast, it's unavoidable when he is tiny but as he gets older, wind him and indulge in a gentle activity, such as looking at a book together before settling him into his cot, to disassociate feeding and sleeping. Try to ensure that he is drowsy but awake enough to be aware of his surroundings. If he is difficult to settle see section 15 – How to settle your baby.

Use the breast as a food supply rather than teaching your baby to become dependent on it as a source of comfort. If your baby uses the breast as a comforter and sleep aid, he will not be able to go to sleep in any other way and as he gets older, your baby may wake regularly between every sleep cycle at night and need you to help him fall back to sleep again.

The exception to this is during the early weeks when you are bonding and establishing milk supply.

> **Don't allow your breast to become a long-term sleep aid.**

" I met up with Stephanie when my baby was 6 months old. As we were talking he started to grizzle and root for milk. Stephanie asked me if he was hungry, I said that he shouldn't be as he had fed 90 minutes ago. She suggested that I put him to the breast so that she could observe, and he immediately started to fall asleep. He was using me as a dummy! That's when I changed my routine and practised a little tough love. I had been finding breastfeeding exhausting as he wanted to be at the breast much of the time and I was

*considering stopping altogether, but once
I weaned him off feeding for comfort
and started to just use the breast
for food, we were both much happier!*

Marilyn, mother of Lucas, aged 6 months.

Create a positive sleep association

Encourage your baby to form an attachment to some sort of comforter. This could be a safe, small soft toy or a small soft cloth square with silky labels attached – you'll work out what is favoured by your baby and, inevitably it will end up having a name such as 'a lovey'. Make sure the item is safe – do not put a large blanket in his cot that he could cover his face with. It's essential to have duplicates so that you can switch them for a wash.

You are aiming for this comforter to become a sleep 'trigger', so each time you place it with your baby he may caress it, rub it between his fingers and become soporific. This is what your baby will turn to for comfort in the middle of the night when he wakes briefly between sleep cycles and it will help him to self-soothe. Current SIDS guidelines advise that you should not place soft toys or anything that could cover your baby's face or head in the cot in the first 12 months but you can familiarise your baby with it before then keeping it against your skin to give it a comforting, reassuring smell and then give it to your baby to hold when you are having a cuddle. Once he is old enough to have his comforter at sleep times, place it in his hand as you lay him in his cot. Not all babies form an attachment with a comforter but when they do it can become a strong and positive sleep association which is portable, always giving your baby a feeling of comfort and security.

> **Encourage a loving attachment**
> **with a comforter or 'lovey'.**
> **Only give the comforter to your baby at sleep**
> **and nap times or it may lose its magic!**

8. Teach the difference between night and day

A newborn baby does not know the difference between night and day, he is simply governed by hunger. In fact, newborns are often on an opposite rhythm to you because while in the womb they are rocked and soothed to sleep all day with your movement and voice, and at night, while you are lying still, they wake. It can take a little time to reverse that pattern.

However, from as early as a couple of weeks old, you can help your baby to learn to distinguish night from day by doing the following:

During the day

★ **Make sure you interact and play with your baby frequently throughout the day.**

★ **Ensure your baby is exposed to plenty of fresh air and daylight by going out for walks or just being out in the garden or the park.**

★ **Don't minimise noise around the house. Carry on as normal so your baby gets used to everyday sounds, like the radio, vacuum cleaner, telephone, etc.**

★ **Draw the curtains when he naps in his room, but don't feel the need to use blackout blinds.**

★ **During the first month, don't let him sleep for longer than 3-4 hours without a feed. Gently guide him into taking more calories during the daytime.**

During the night

★ **Have a predictable bedtime routine with sleep cues.**

★ **Keep lights low while preparing for bedtime as bright lights suppress the production of melatonin, the sleep hormone.**

★ **Change him into night-time clothing or use a baby sleeping bag.**

★ **Draw curtains and use blackout blinds if you have them.**

★ **Make sure his room is warm and cosy, but not too hot, and check for draughts.**

★ **Make night feeds short, keeping the light as low as possible and stay in the bedroom.**

★ **Do not play or chat with your baby, just whisper and keep interaction to a minimum.**

★ **Avoid eye contact and do not engage with your baby.**

You need to be a very different person when you tend to your baby in the night compared to during the day. Be boring! Avoid interaction and keep your voice low. In the morning throw open the curtains, smile and totally engage using your happy daytime voice.

> **Be boring during the night!**

9. Demand feeding

Demand feeding means feeding your baby whenever he signals that he's hungry, usually by crying, rooting or sucking on his hands, rather than according to a set schedule.

By all means, demand feed your baby but do not feed at every demand!

Let me elaborate... In the early days and weeks while you are establishing your milk supply and bonding with your baby you will need to breastfeed little and often. This will help your milk supply, encourage bonding with your baby and help him to learn the technique to take a good feed. Your baby has a tiny tummy and cannot take in large volumes so will have to feed frequently.

Likewise, if you are bottle feeding, feed your baby when he shows signs of hunger and let him feed as long as he wants to. In the early days, this will be little and often. You will learn to recognise his hunger cues and his 'hungry' cry.

However, once feeding is established, after the first month or so, start to space your feeds gradually. If you are feeding 2 hourly, increase to 2.25 hourly for a couple of days, then 2.5 hourly and so on. Once your baby is able to take bigger feeds, less often, this will help him to sleep for longer periods during the night.

As your baby gets older if you allow him to constantly 'snack feed' he is unlikely to take enough food to sustain him through naps of a restorative length and if he snack feeds during the day he will want to snack feed at regular intervals at night. If you are breastfeeding, encourage your baby to take a full feed as your milk gradually increases in fat and calorific content during a feed and is therefore likely to satisfy your baby for longer. For this reason, it is important not to switch breasts while your baby is actively nursing.

Do not meet every emotional need with food

In a world where obesity is on the increase, we must be aware not to meet every need or quell any cry with food. Babies cry for all manner of reasons – they're wet, they're tired, they're in pain, they're bored – so it's important to establish why your baby is crying and what he needs. I often talk to parents of older babies who say their child never cries. I actually believe that you need to allow your baby to cry or shout to understand their needs. If you always meet their cry with a breast to nurse on or a bottle of milk to keep them quiet, then they may grow up feeling that food is the answer to every emotional need.

Feeding for every emotional need is not a good life lesson for your baby. If you teach your baby that when he's bored he gets fed, when he is uncomfortable he gets fed and so on this may follow in later life and food may become a source of comfort, resulting in an unhealthy relationship with food.

> **Assess your baby's needs; don't just assume he is hungry.**

10. Let your baby have a voice

Crying is your baby's only form of communication. Pause, observe and listen. If you quell every cry, how can you understand what your baby is trying to tell you?

★ **Is he hungry?**
★ **Is he bored?**
★ **Is he uncomfortable?**
★ **Does he have wind?**
★ **Does he need a nappy change?**
★ **Is he too hot/too cold?**
★ **Is he unwell?**
★ **Is he trying to connect sleep cycles? This may often involve a little crying or grizzling.**

Try to differentiate between his cries. Babies have different cries for different needs. Is he actually crying because he's distressed and hungry or is he letting off some steam and trying to settle himself to sleep?

One of the most valuable things you have taught me is simply to "allow my baby her voice". Before you said that to me, I was always desperate to find the quickest way to stop her from crying. Now I understand that sometimes she just needs to cry and I've learnt to differentiate her cries much better.

Toni, mother of Willow, aged 5 months.

11. The pause

I think 'pausing' is a very important part of understanding your baby. Don't react to him too quickly; pause, observe and listen. If your baby is ever going to learn to connect his sleep cycles independently you have to give him the opportunity to do so! If you pick him up the moment he cries, you may even be waking him.

I am not saying let your baby wail or cry in distress, absolutely not, just listen, assess and don't rush in as soon as he stirs. Babies can be very noisy when learning how to connect sleep cycles; it may involve some crying, moaning or grumbling.

Babies are often noisy sleepers and because current guidelines recommend that your baby sleeps in your room until 6 months of age, it is very easy for a parent to react too quickly to their baby's cry because they don't want their partner to be disturbed. This is understandable if one parent has an early start and a long day of work ahead, but these quick reactions can actually wake the baby when, if he were left for a few minutes, he may have resettled himself. Rushing to his every stir or grizzle means you are basically connecting his sleep cycles for him, never allowing him the opportunity to learn to self-settle, which will subsequently encourage regular waking. If his grizzle becomes a cry of need, you then, of course, attend to him. Allowing a pause will help in the long term so ask your partner to read this and bear with you! If one of the parents is working with machinery or doing a lot of driving, you may wish to consider sleeping in separate bedrooms for the first few weeks.

Parents of second and subsequent children often say that their babies are more contented and better sleepers than the first. This is usually because the carer is busier and more distracted and therefore gives the second child the opportunity to learn to self-settle and connect his own sleep cycles.

> **Give your baby the opportunity to learn to connect their sleep cycles independently.**

> **"** *I do feel that putting into practice the lessons you taught me has helped already, even though Olivia is only 4 weeks old. You have given me the confidence to take a step back and pause to see exactly what she is crying about and whether she is just trying to get herself to sleep, which she actually often does.* **"**

Serena, mother of Olivia, aged 4 weeks.

12. Feeding at night

When you feed your baby during the night, you do not need to wake him before putting him back down to sleep (this is only essential at the start of the night). Give the feed, either breast or bottle, keep interaction to a minimum, wind and settle back in to the cot as quickly as possible. Only change the nappy during the night if absolutely necessary.

As your baby gets older, don't always assume he needs a night feed, when he wakes. If he fed 2 hours ago, he doesn't need feeding again. Simply resettle him. It may be difficult at first, but with consistency it will get easier, your baby will soon learn that you are not going to feed him every 2 hours during the night.

As a new parent it can be difficult to know how often to feed. In the early weeks, if you are 'demand' feeding, your baby may feed little and often. However, if you are feeding 3 hourly during the day and he is waking hourly at night, a feed is probably not the answer and your baby may just need some comfort and help to resettle.

Bottle fed babies can often settle into a more structured routine early on, but with a breastfed baby it can be more difficult as you cannot be certain of how much milk your baby has taken at a particular feed. It can really help to keep a diary of feeds, and if your baby is feeding every 3 or 4 hours in the day, they should not need to feed more often than that at night. If they are settling independently at the start of the night they should sleep for longer and longer stretches during the night, naturally dropping night feeds and only rousing between sleep cycles if they are genuinely hungry.

> **If your baby wakes in the night, don't always assume he needs a feed, he may just need some help resettling.**

Dream feeds

Many parenting advisors recommend 'dream feeding' your baby at around 10 or 11 p.m. before the parents go to bed. As the name suggests, this involves feeding your baby while he is still asleep. The theory is that by doing this the parents 'hopefully' get to have a longer stretch of uninterrupted sleep when they themselves are in their deep sleep phase.

I have mixed feelings about this. I feel that by dream feeding you are interrupting your baby's natural rhythms, disturbing his sleep pattern development and are feeding him when he is not hungry. Moreover, at around 10 or 11 p.m., your baby is in his deep non-REM sleep phase, a time of important physical development so I do not feel you should stimulate the digestive system when it wants to rest.

By dream feeding you're in danger of creating a learnt hunger in your baby at that time. Whereas if you allow your baby's natural rhythms to develop, the length of time he sleeps should gradually increase, especially during this period of deep sleep where he should find it easier to connect his sleep cycles.

In my mind, a much better solution is for the parents to have an early night so that they can achieve a decent period of deep sleep before being woken. Remember, this difficult period of adjusting to your baby's sleep patterns is such a short time in the grand scheme of things, that a little compromise on your part as a parent can really pay dividends in the long term.

How to wean your baby off night feeds

At around 6 months old, your baby should no longer need milk during the night, provided he is feeding well in the day and is in good health. Feeding during the night stimulates his metabolism at a time when he should be resting. If you have taught him to self-settle from a young age he may well have stopped waking for feeds long ago. If he is still waking this is a learnt habit which can be changed.

Regular night feeding also creates a negative cycle where your baby is filling up on calories during the night so is not needing to eat so much in the day. Once you wean off night feeds, you should see his appetite improve during the day. If you have a particularly hungry baby, your baby has medical issues or if you have any doubts, consult your GP or health visitor before reducing night feeds.

If your baby has learnt to self-settle at the start of the night you can gently and gradually eliminate night feeds. If your baby is still feeding to sleep at the start of the night you need to address this issue before attempting to cut out night feeds. See section 15 – How to settle your baby.

There are two techniques to reduce night feeding. The first is to decrease the amount of milk you are giving your baby at each feed. For a bottle fed baby, gradually reduce the volume of milk given over a period of nights. For example, you can reduce the volume by half to 1 fl oz (15–30 ml), each night until you reach 2 fl oz and then stop altogether and use a settling technique (see section 15) to help your baby get back to sleep. For a breastfed baby, gradually reduce the amount of minutes offered at the breast over a period of nights and once you are down to a couple of minutes, stop altogether and use a settling technique.

The second technique is to increase the interval between feeds. For example, if your baby is feeding every 3 hours, increase the time between feeds to 3.5 hours for two nights and then 4 hourly for two nights and so on.

Choose one method or the other, you do not need to do both. Your baby should gradually wake less for milk and eventually give it up altogether; if not, you will need to implement a settling technique to help him get back to sleep, as described in section 15. However, your baby should have gradually adjusted to eating less during the night so is less likely to experience hunger and his appetite should improve during the day.

As I have said before, it's crucial that you are consistent. Once you have stopped night feeding, do not go back to it! This will confuse your baby. If he wakes during the night because, for example, he is teething, or is unwell, give him love, comfort, cuddles, water if necessary and any medication that a health professional has recommended but don't feed him for comfort. If you are tempted to feed him to get him back to sleep, you'll be disrupting all the good work you have done to wean him off his night feeds, and this will affect his appetite during the day, once again creating a negative cycle and confusion.

Also, do not be lured into feeding him to keep him quiet in other tricky situations, such as when you are on holiday and his sleep patterns have been slightly disrupted, or when you're staying with friends and you feel awkward about him potentially waking the household. It may seem like the easy option at the time but it is unfair on your baby, and will cause confusion.

> **The golden rules are time, repetition and consistency.**

13. Routine

Babies love routine! Once your baby is around 6 to 8 weeks old try to establish a regular daytime feed and nap routine to avoid your baby becoming overtired. Learn your baby's rhythms and establish a routine tailored to your lifestyle and situation.

Keep a note of when your baby sleeps and for how long; this will help you to understand your baby's rhythm. If you keep nap times regular your baby will get used to sleeping at that time and he will find it easier to fall asleep. I don't believe in a rigid feeding and sleeping routine, I think there needs to be some flexibility, but I do think that babies who have a routine are often more content and so are their parents. Instead of clock watching, try to think of it as a sequence of events with a consistent pattern and work at your baby's pace.

This is not an exact science, all babies differ but here are some guidelines:

6-12 weeks – A nap every 2 hours.

3-6 months – A nap every 2-3 hours.

6-9 months – Three naps. In the morning, one sleep cycle (approximately 45-60 minutes). Lunch time, two sleep cycles (approximately 90 minutes). Afternoon, one sleep cycle or catnap, depending on age, waking no later than 4-4.30p.m. (dependent on bedtime). Babies are often difficult to settle for this afternoon nap, so this could be a nap triggered by you taking them for a stroll in the pushchair.

9–12 months – Two naps. You can now drop the late afternoon nap. Morning, one sleep cycle. Post lunch, two sleep cycles, waking no later than 3.30 p.m.

12 months plus – You can now work towards one nap a day. Some babies will do this earlier than others, but when you feel they are ready (usually between 12 and 18 months), you may need to bring lunch time forward to 11.30 a.m. for a transitional period and then put baby down for a long nap straight after, aiming at 2 hours. Once your baby has adjusted to this new routine you can gradually move lunch back to your usual time.

2–3 years – Your child will probably have one lunchtime nap of 1–1.5 hours at this time, shortening as they get nearer to 3 years, although some will completely drop their nap before the age of three. However, you need to try to avoid your child becoming so overtired that he drops off late afternoon, as a late sleep will affect bedtime.

3 years plus – Although a nap isn't usually necessary at this age, I think it's good to encourage a quiet period after lunch, maybe reading stories or listening to story CDs.

> **Learn your baby's rhythms.**

Once I got my twins into a manageable routine, I began to enjoy them so much more, they became happier, generally more contented and I got a little time to myself too!

Rachel, mother of Toby and Zoe, aged 8 months.

Feeding and napping routine

Establish a routine which does not involve feeding just before napping. This is key! You do not want your baby to develop a feed-to-sleep association so I would recommend feeding your baby shortly after he has woken from his nap rather than just before he goes back down for his next nap. This has the added advantage that it should encourage your baby to take a good, full feed as he won't be falling asleep while feeding. A positive sleep/awake pattern to follow is:

Nap
Feed
Play/interaction
Nap

If you must feed just before your baby is due a nap, do not feed-to-sleep. If baby is dropping off, tickle his feet, wind him and maybe have a look at a picture book or sing a lullaby to break the association between feeding and sleeping, and then put baby in his cot or Moses basket, drowsy but awake. If your older baby is hungry at nap time try giving him milk from a beaker to avoid him sucking to sleep.

Once feeding is well established or by at least 2 months old try to elongate the time between feeds. If you are feeding 2 hourly, gradually move on to 3 hourly, by increasing the interval between feeds by 15 minutes every couple of days until you reach the desired time between feeds. If your baby feeds every 2 hours or less he will only be able to take a small feed each time which will not sustain him through his next nap but by gradually extending this time he will be able to take a bigger and more satisfying feed. This will help him to sleep longer at night too. When you feel he is ready, you can move on to 4 hourly feeds. Do what works best for you and your baby.

Having fallen into the trap of nursing my first baby to sleep, I found it really difficult to settle her in any other way and I didn't want to do the same again.

Therefore, with my second daughter, I chose a pattern of feeding shortly after waking rather than just before a nap. This was so much easier as my daughter didn't associate feeding with sleeping. Quite early on, I also worked towards establishing an organised but flexible feeding and napping schedule. This helped me to fit in with my older daughter's activities and my baby was generally more contented and a much better sleeper than my first.

Amelia, mother of Sophia, aged three and Maisie, aged 9 months.

Bath/bed routine

If you haven't established a bath/bed routine by the time your baby is 3 months old, then this is the ideal time to implement it.

A regular and predictable bath routine is essential. It relaxes your baby and helps melatonin levels to rise. This is the sleep hormone discussed in section 4, which will help your baby settle more easily. A routine also creates cues to help your baby to understand the difference between night-time and daytime sleep. Babies learn by association so quickly get used to a repetitive pattern.

★ **Your routine should commence at the same time every night and should take no longer than 30–45 minutes. If you make your routine longer than this, your baby will lose focus and you will not benefit from the melatonin rise.**

★ **Plan your routine around a time that fits in with your family life and other children. For example, there is no point in bathing your baby, having him all warm, cosy and drowsy and then dad comes home from work and wants to play. You will lose all the advantages you have gained and your baby will probably go to bed overtired and overstimulated.**

★ **Avoid exposing your baby to TV or computer screens in the early evening as the blue lights from such devices inhibit the production of melatonin.**

★ **Around 7 p.m. for bedtime, or a little earlier, seems to fit in with many families so that would mean commencing your routine around 6.15 to 6.30 but having quiet time before then.**

From around 4 months of age, it's best to give your baby his last feed before his bath, this way, you are completely disassociating feeding and sleeping. This can also be helpful for colicky/windy babies as it enables the baby to get his wind up before settling to sleep. If you avoid giving a full feed after bath your baby is less likely to fall asleep on the breast or bottle. Once your baby is used to this routine it works very well, however some parents feel this goes against instinct and worry that bathing with a full stomach will be uncomfortable for their baby, but remember this night-time bath should be short, calming and relaxing, so this really isn't an issue. An alternative compromise is to do a split feed; give half before and half after bath, but if you do this, ensure your baby does not fall asleep while feeding and read a story or sing a lullaby between feeding and putting into the cot to create a gap between food and sleep.

Give your baby a warm, soothing and quiet, short bath, rather than a playful experience. After the bath, wrap baby in a towel, and give him a massage if you like, then dress him in night clothes and take him into the bedroom. When you take your baby out of his warm bath, he experiences a temperature drop and this creates a boost of melatonin. Do not go back to the living area, as this will stimulate your baby. Have the lights low in the bedroom and quietly look at a book or sing a lullaby together. Your routine can be whatever you want it to be as long as it's quiet and gentle. The most important thing is that you do the same every night. Make it predictable so baby understands it's bedtime.

Remember, we are aiming for drowsy but awake! If you play soothing music during your routine, turn it off now and place your baby in his cot, say soothing words and explain that it's sleep time. Soothe if necessary, but for your baby to sleep well he needs to learn to fall asleep independently, without your presence.

Remember to ensure that the conditions he falls asleep in are the conditions he will find himself in when he rouses during the night. For example – don't play music: when he rouses, it will be silent; don't leave a light on and then turn it off later: when he rouses, it will be dark. A low plug-in night light is ideal so you can see if you need to attend to him.

> **Put your baby into his cot drowsy but awake.**

> *My baby often cries himself to sleep but it's a grizzle rather than a cry of distress. I give him 5 minutes or so and if he hasn't settled I check on him in case he has a bit of wind or a dirty nappy.*

Sarah, mother of Max, aged 4 months.

Sleep cue words

When you put your baby down for a sleep, during the day, night or in the middle of the night, say the same reassuring words from day one. Something like, 'Night

night, my darling, it's sleep time now. I love you,' and give a kiss and a cuddle. Sleep cue words are powerful and reassuring, get your partner, child-minder, nanny, whoever, to use the same words.

14. Naps

Daytime naps are so important. Do not let anyone tell you that if your baby sleeps in the day he won't sleep at night, the opposite is true! Naps are a good teaching time and sleep encourages sleep. If your baby is well rested he will find it easier to go to sleep at night, will be more content and have a healthier appetite. If you restrict naps, your baby will be overtired, cortisol levels will increase (see section 4 – Sleep hormones) and he may find it difficult to get to sleep and be more prone to night waking and early rising.

Create a mini-nap routine with sleep cues. For example, after some gentle quiet play or lullabies, go to your baby's nursery, read a short story and settle him into his cot, gently explaining that it's sleep time. Parents quite often have difficulty in getting their babies to nap in their cots during the day and end up taking them for a walk or a drive at every nap time. This is acceptable in the short term for creating a regular sleep pattern but try to encourage a sleep in the cot or Moses basket at least once a day. If your baby is not keen, be persistent and keep trying.

The secret to good napping is getting the spacing between each nap right. This is where a sleep diary is beneficial. It will help you to understand your baby's rhythms. Look for sleep cues, which are sometimes very subtle and don't wait until your baby is overtired to put him down for a nap.

Sleep cues

* **Staring**
* **Loss of interest in people and toys**
* **Decreased activity**
* **Less vocal**
* **Burying his face into your chest**
* **Rubbing eyes**
* **Pulling ears**
* **Yawning and stretching**
* **Whining and crying**

If you put your baby down for his first nap of the day too early you may encourage early rising, if you put him down too late in the day, you may have problems at bedtime, as your baby will be less likely to be tired.

During the day, babies sleep in approximately 45 minute sleep cycles so you will probably find that naps are either around 45 minutes or 90 minutes long.

Anything less than 45 minutes does not provide your baby with the full physiological benefits that deeper sleep offers so if your baby is having lots of catnaps or short naps, he is not having fully restorative sleep. Try to encourage fewer but longer naps. Make adjustments gradually, if you try to space naps too rapidly, your baby will become overtired and grumpy. A good rule of thumb is to aim to move on by 15 minutes every couple of days.

Remember, any adjustments you make will take time to kick in. Don't make changes and after two or three days, think, 'this is not working, I'll change it'. You will end up with a very confused baby.

TIME, REPETITION AND CONSISTENCY are key!

If you find your baby difficult to settle for naps, see section 15 – How to settle your baby.

Sleep encourages sleep!

15. How to settle your baby

The younger your baby, the easier it is to teach them to self-settle.

0-2 months – Anything goes! This is a time for bonding and getting to know your baby. He may need a lot of comfort and cuddles in these early weeks along with help to settle and connect his sleep cycles. However, do give him the opportunity to sleep in his cot or Moses basket. Although it's lovely to hold a sleeping baby, your baby needs to feel comfortable in his own space so giving early opportunities for this will be beneficial in the long term.

2–3 months – Don't be scared to settle your baby in his cot or Moses basket for sleeps. He may enjoy sleeping in your arms, which is fine some of the time but the kindest thing you can do at this age is to teach him to fall asleep in his own space. So when he is ready for a nap, has a clean nappy and is not hungry, settle him into his cot, say your reassuring sleep words and put a firm comforting hand on him, then step back and leave him to self-settle, he may cry a little, if this crying escalates try to soothe him with some shushing and patting. If the crying continues to escalate, pick him up and comfort him, once he is calm but before he is asleep lay him down and start the process again. This is what's known as a trust technique, if you continue to do this until he is asleep, you are giving the message: 'I'm here for you, I will respond to you and I will love and comfort you but I want you to go to sleep in your cot.' If you pick him up and rock him to sleep when he cries you are reinforcing the crying and teaching him that the louder and longer you cry, I will rock you to sleep. Be positive and confident and try to encourage both parents to settle him especially if you are a breastfeeding mum, so dad is actively involved and your baby doesn't get dependent on only mum settling him.

3-6 months – If you have not taught your baby to self-settle before now you may have to be a little more persistent, but if you are consistent it will pay off. As above, try to settle him in his cot, say your reassuring sleep words, and put a comforting firm hand on him. Walk away but if your baby's crying escalates to more than a grizzle or sleepy cry, go back to him and shush, pat and comfort. The crucial thing is to see it through until sleep is achieved. However much your baby protests, just stay with him, continue to settle him, almost cuddle him in his cot if you have to. Try to resist picking him up, but if you feel you need to, once he is calm and before he is asleep, lay him back down and start again. You MUST see this through until sleep is achieved. You are not abandoning him to his cries and he will not feel unloved as you are staying with him. Do the same at every sleep situation and each time he achieves sleep in this way, however long it takes, it will be easier the next time. If you are consistent with this you will be amazed how quickly the teaching process is but I must stress that you have to see it through. If you give up, you reinforce crying.

This is what's known as a **gradual retreat** process, so once your baby is comfortable to go to sleep with your help and soothing, you need to move to the next degree of separation as we don't want him to form an inappropriate sleep association, and become dependent on your presence to get to sleep. Your next step will be to use less intervention, so less patting and soothing, maybe just an occasional pat and shush. The retreat continues until you are ready to just sit next to his cot if necessary.

If you are teaching this from a young age you will move through the steps more quickly. Be mindful that your goal is to teach your baby to settle without your presence so you are aiming to lay him in his cot after a cuddle, say night, night and leave the room. For more information on gradual retreat, see section 20 – Sleep teaching techniques.

It is very difficult to put a timescale on how long this process will take. It will depend on how old your baby is and whether you have always cuddled, rocked or fed him to sleep in the past. Some babies will respond quicker than others so it could take three or four days or it could take two or three weeks, for you to be able to settle him and then leave the room. In some cases, your presence may be over-stimulating so it might be more beneficial to just leave your baby to settle himself. However, the most important thing is to be consistent and not change tack after a few nights, this will just confuse your baby.

Remember that babies can be noisy when settling. It may involve 5 minutes of crying – lots of babies cry themselves to sleep but this is not a cry of distress. Listen and learn your baby's cries. They may just be a bit cross, or are maybe just letting off a bit of steam and tension, this is normal, only intervene if your baby is distressed.

Nap times are good for teaching self-settling. Choose your baby's most predictable nap, the one where he usually settles the easiest. This is usually the morning nap. Avoid the late afternoon nap as this is often when they find settling more difficult and are more likely to just catnap.

If your baby is struggling to settle, think about the following:

★ **Is he hungry?**
★ **Is he overtired?**
★ **Is he under-tired?**
★ **Does he have wind?**
★ **Does he have a dirty nappy?**
★ **He may have abdominal discomfort and need a bowel movement?**
★ **Is he too hot/too cold?**
★ **Is he feeling unwell/teething?**

> *Once I had taught Alex to self-settle, I could just put him down in his cot and he would go to sleep! He would sometimes have a shout or a grizzle but he knew it was sleepy time. I felt a great sense of achievement.*
>
> Jan, mother of Alex, aged 6 months.

Swaddling

Swaddling is the technique of snuggly wrapping your baby in a cotton sheet, or specially designed swaddling wrap. It can give your baby a feeling of security and may help to trigger sleep in the first few weeks. It can also prevent your baby waking himself up with the Moro reflex, also known as the 'startle reflex'. This is an involuntary response which is present for the first 3 to 6 months.

I swaddled my triplets and found it to be a very effective sleep cue. I think that multiples often respond well to swaddling as it mirrors the sensation of the womb. From birth, after swaddle wrapping my babies, I lay them in their Moses baskets and allowed them to self-settle as I simply had no time to rock them to sleep! However, not all babies enjoy being swaddled.

If you decide to swaddle, ensure that you do not swaddle too tightly around the legs and hips as this can cause hip dysplasia (problems with the hips), your baby's legs need to be able to move into a natural 'frog-like' position. Do not use a blanket as your baby may overheat, ensure your baby's face is not covered and follow safe practice guidelines which you can find on the internet at www.nct.org.uk and www.babycentre.co.uk.

If your baby is premature or has any medical conditions, take advice from your paediatrician on swaddling.

Monitors

A monitor will allow you to listen to or see your baby when you are in another room. Some also have sensor pads which detect breathing and movement. There is a vast range on the market so you will need to research the options within your budget.

More and more families I work with have camera monitors now. Before I had seen them in use, I would have thought it an unnecessary expense but I must say I think they are excellent. It allows parents to watch and assess whether intervention is needed. As I've said many times already, babies can be quite noisy and move around quite a lot while connecting their sleep cycles or self-settling. If you are just focusing on listening it can sound quite loud and you may well go in and wake a sleeping baby. Sometimes you will watch a baby crying on the monitor but their eyes are actually closed, this is all part of their self-soothing process. So I think this is a good investment and rather than making you over attentive I think it gives you the confidence to pause and give your baby an opportunity to settle.

> *Having a camera monitor has made me a much less jumpy mummy. With my first baby I think I used to disturb her by going to check on her unnecessarily each time she stirred or grumbled. The video gives me the confidence to wait and observe to see if my intervention is actually necessary.*
>
> Liz, mother of Harriet, aged 5 months.

16. Twins, triplets and more

As a mother of triplets, I would say the key thing that worked for me was routine, routine, routine!

I belong to a very active and supportive group of triplet and quad mums and depending on the birth weight of our babies, the majority of us have followed a 3–4 hourly feeding schedule, whether breast or bottle feeding. Babies can be fed in tandem or one after the other. Obviously if you have help it is much easier, but not all of us have that luxury so it can be quite a juggling act.

This system of scheduled feeding may not be right for you if you have babies of very different weights or with medical issues, in which case you will need to be guided by your paediatrician. It is helpful to keep a daily feed and sleep diary for each baby.

Try to create a consistent pattern of feeding and sleeping and once they have reached a healthy weight, if your health visitor or paediatrician is in agreement you can allow them to sleep for longer periods at night. If one wakes to feed, I would suggest you feed them all to keep them in a consistent pattern.

Establish a set bedtime for your babies, and don't worry too much about them waking each other. Multiples generally don't seem to be bothered by their siblings' cries. Mine could certainly sleep through each other's cries which always amazed me!

As a parent of multiples I think you are less likely to fall in to sleep problems as you simply don't have the time to rock or feed to sleep, so babies tend to learn to self-settle at an earlier age. Once babies self-settle they are more likely to drop their night feeds of their own accord as they learn to soothe themselves back to sleep between sleep cycles and only wake if they are genuinely hungry.

You can choose to sleep your multiples in the same cot (co-bedding) or allow them to sleep in separate cots in the same room. Research has shown that sleeping similarly sized multiples in the same cot can help them to synchronise their sleep cycles. If you decide to co-bed, it is essential that you follow the safe co-bedding guidelines available through The Twins and Multiple Births Association (www.tamba.org.uk).

The early weeks will be very tiring so try to sleep when your babies sleep, and even if you only have time for a 'power nap' in the day, you will feel better for it. If your babies cots don't fit in your room, set up a bed in their room and if you have a partner, take turns in doing the night feeds, when possible.

Young babies can often get very fractious in the early evening, needing extra cuddles and soothing. If possible, try to get some help at this time, however if you are alone, simple bouncy chairs are helpful as you can rock them with your feet while simultaneously soothing another baby. I personally wouldn't recommend the vibrating chairs as these can create an unhelpful sleep trigger/association.

Try to get out at least once a day, as light and fresh air help to develop your babies biological day/night cycles. I don't think I left the house for the first month but after that my afternoon stroll with my babies was my absolute sanity saver!

Caring for multiples is exhausting so do accept offers of help and don't try to go it alone. Local colleges may offer childcare students on placement, I couldn't have managed without student help. There is also a charity called 'Homestart' that can offer help and support in some parts of the country (www.home-start.org.uk).

My triplets were born at 35 weeks, we came out of hospital 12 days later and by this time I was feeding 3 hourly. They were very sleepy so it wasn't difficult to establish this. I breastfed two of them fully and one had breast milk supplemented with formula due to weight loss. I breastfed to a schedule as I felt that this was the only way I could manage to feed them all. We soon went on to 4 hourly feeding and it's ingrained in my mind that I fed them at 10, 2 and 6, both a.m. and p.m. I wasn't encouraged to breastfeed by the health professionals in hospital, I was even told that it wasn't possible to breastfeed triplets, however, I had done my research and I knew it was possible. I had one very supportive nurse in the special care unit who said if you are going to do this you need to teach your babies to feed to a schedule and take their feed quickly! She was right, for us, this worked and it was a very positive experience. The babies rhythms were governed by their feeding schedule, I could almost set my clock to the 2 a.m. feed. At night my husband would get the babies up, change nappies, if necessary, and I would stay in bed and feed, the first two in tandem and then the third. We got so proficient at doing the night feed, that we could have them all fed and all be back asleep within the hour!

17. Early rising

I feel the need to dedicate a section to early rising as it is a common problem that can be exhausting for parents and one that can be difficult to resolve.

I would suggest that you treat any time before 6 a.m. as night-time, depending on what time your baby goes to sleep at the start of the night. However, if your baby is regularly waking at 5 a.m. and not settling back to sleep you need to try to establish the reason for this.

There are four common reasons for early rising. These are:

1. Baby is being rewarded for early waking and will therefore persist in waking as he enjoys the contact. Rewards can come in various shapes:

★ **Feeding at the early wake-up time, which can become a learnt hunger and perpetuate the early waking. SOLUTION – Avoid feeding at this time and instead use one of the settling techniques described in section 15 – How to settle your baby.**
★ **Giving him your full attention at that time, so as not to disturb the rest of the family.**

SOLUTION – As you have read earlier, minimal attention is more effective at night-time. You need to leave your baby to entertain himself and if you are consistent, he will learn that his waking will not be rewarded. Once you have reached an acceptable wake up time, go to him, and using your happy daytime voice, open the curtains, make a fuss of him and start the day.

★ Taking him into bed with you, so as not to disturb the rest of the family. This is a fabulous reward for early rising so your baby will definitely continue to do so!

SOLUTION – You need to stop taking him into your bed and help him to resettle by using the techniques described above. Be prepared that your baby will cry and protest as you have previously taught him that the more he protests the more likely you are to reward him so you need to re-teach. If you are consistent he will learn that his early waking will not be rewarded and he will gradually start to sleep later. If necessary, you may need to use a settling technique from section 20, or with an older baby you may leave him to protest, maybe with a couple of soft toys to entertain him. This will call for a little tough love and some disturbed mornings for all the family but it will pay dividends in the long term.

2. Timing of daytime naps – If the first nap of the day is too early and too long, this will be compensating for the early rising. Ideally, if your baby is over 6 months old the first nap of the day will be around 9 a.m. and should be for around 45–60 minutes with a longer nap at lunchtime. If your baby is napping too early, rather than suddenly moving his nap forwards and risking him become overtired, move the morning nap forwards by 15 minutes every two days until you reach the desired time.

3. Early sleep phase – If your baby is going to sleep very early in the evening, he is likely to wake early in the morning. For example, if he goes to sleep at 6 p.m. and wakes at 5 a.m., he has achieved a solid 11 hours of sleep and is therefore unlikely to resettle easily. To help him to readjust his body clock you need to help him to shift this whole period of night-time sleep forwards. You are more likely to succeed if you do this gradually to allow his body clock to accommodate the change. A more desirable sleep phase would be 7 p.m. to 6 a.m., therefore move bedtime forwards by 15 minutes every couple of nights until you reach the desired time, moving meal times and daytime naps accordingly. It may take 2–4 weeks for his body clock to adjust.

4. Light – Ensure there is no daylight filtering around the side of the curtains as light suppresses the sleep hormone, melatonin and will therefore contribute to early waking. It is worth investing in blackout blinds. Portable ones are also available and worth considering when going on holiday.

18. Times of change

There are many developmental changes and physical factors that can affect your baby's sleep. These are often referred to as 'sleep regressions' but actually they are a time of developmental progress for your child. You may have got into a lovely predictable routine and then it all changes. During these periods of intense development you may need to spend more time settling your baby to help him to feel secure as he goes through these developmental stages. For example:

★ Growth spurts – **your baby's sleeping and waking patterns are influenced by hunger as well as their circadian rhythm so while he is going through a growth spurt he may wake more regularly to feed. Growth spurts can happen any time during the first year but common times are between 1 and 3 weeks, 6 and 8 weeks, 3 months, 6 months and 9 months.**

★ Circadian rhythm changes – the circadian rhythm is the 24-hour sequence of biological cycles which influence patterns of sleeping, waking, rest, hunger, activity, body temperature and hormones. Various factors can influence this, such as the length of sleep cycles extending as your baby matures; your baby being able to sleep for longer periods without feeding; the development of non-REM sleep.

★ Teething – this can be disruptive to sleep and some babies experience more discomfort than others. There are various things you can do to alleviate the pain and along with traditional medication there are homeopathic remedies available. To prevent your baby from becoming dependent on your prolonged presence at night, try to deal with him in a quiet and straightforward way, avoiding bringing him into bed with you and aim to get your normal routine back on track as soon as possible. If this does cause sleep problems, you may have to follow a gradual retreat process when he is well again. See section 15 – How to settle your baby.

★ Separation anxiety – this can start between the ages of 6 to 12 months. However, if you stay with your baby while he falls asleep, he will become dependent on your presence so a better solution is to return regularly to comfort and reassure him until he falls asleep. See Part 4 – Sleep Solutions.

★ **4-month sleep regression – As your baby's brain matures, his sleep pattern will change, and because of this at around 3–4 months many parents experience sleep problems, commonly termed 'the 4-month sleep regression'. If you follow the tips and advice in this book, you will never experience this!**

★ Ability to stay awake at will **– avoid putting stimulating toys in your baby's cot as this will perpetuate this problem.**

★ Gross motor skills development **– ability to sit up/ stand up/crawl. At around 8–12 months your baby's sleep may be disrupted when he starts to move around his cot, roll over, sit up and in particular when he learns to stand up against the side of his cot. This is especially problematic when he can stand up but cannot lower himself back down again. Try to help him to develop this skill by playing some daytime games where he lifts and lowers himself. If you have to lay him down at night, keep interaction to a minimum to avoid this becoming a game.**

★ Change in circumstances **– external factors can also affect sleep, like a new sibling, moving house, going on holiday, particularly to a different time zone, starting nursery or going to a childminder. You may need to give your baby extra comfort at these times and once he is settled gradually withdraw your presence. See Part 4 – Sleep Solutions.**

★ Clock change – this is a time that many parents dread, particularly in the autumn when the clocks go back, which can cause an early riser to wake even earlier! You can either choose to 'go with the flow' and allow your baby or child's body clock to adapt naturally or you can tweak your baby's schedule ahead of time. You do this by pushing bedtime forwards or backwards by 15 minutes every few days until bedtime has moved by one hour and hopefully the wake up time will adapt accordingly. You will also need to adjust naps, meal and milk times during the day.

★ Illness – if your baby is sleeping in his own bedroom and you need to monitor him due to illness, it is better to move a mattress on to the floor of his room, rather than bring him into your room to sleep. This will help avoid confusion and once he is better it will be easier to get back on track with his normal routine.

During times of change it can be really helpful to keep a sleep diary as this will help you to understand your baby's rhythms and you can adjust his routine accordingly. When you are writing a sleep diary, it is particularly useful to note how long it takes your baby to get to sleep, it should take no longer than 10 to 15 minutes. If it takes longer he may be under-tired or overtired and the easiest way to understand this is to look back over your diary to see what timings seem to be working best for your baby. There is a sleep diary template to fill in at the back of this book.

Part Three

SLEEP SUMMARY: NEWBORN TO 6 MONTHS

Now that you have read about how your baby sleeps and how to establish positive sleep habits, I thought it would be useful to recap on key points at different stages.

0-6 weeks

★ **Anything goes! This is your time for bonding with your baby, getting to know each other and establishing feeding. If you are breastfeeding you will need to feed regularly to establish your milk supply.**

★ **Your newborn baby will not be able to self-settle so will need to be soothed. Some babies need a lot more pacifying than others in these early days.**

★ **Even though it's lovely to cuddle a sleeping baby, occasionally try to put your baby down in his Moses basket or cot, drowsy but awake enough to be aware of his surroundings.**

★ **Try not to over-stimulate your newborn baby. In the first month, the longest time your baby should be awake between naps is 45-60 minutes. Over-stimulation in the early weeks is common, causing your baby to be fractious and can sometimes be misinterpreted as colic. Lots of visitors, being handed from person to person, much interaction and being rocked and jiggled can cause over-stimulation of your baby's sensory nervous system. You may need to consider sending your visitors home and taking your baby to a darkened room to gently soothe and calm him.**

* As your baby gets closer to 6 weeks of age try not to always 'feed to sleep' although this will inevitably happen in the early weeks as feeding will be tiring for him.
* Help your baby to distinguish between night and day.

6-12 weeks

* Work on the timings of your feeds, whether breast or bottle. Try to establish a loosely organised but flexible feeding and sleeping routine, based around your baby's own rhythms.
* Adjust your routine, so you don't feed just before your baby is due a nap or you will create a sleep association and your baby will only know how to go to sleep while feeding, this will result in total dependence and regular night waking in the future.
* Feeding your baby after a nap will also ensure that he has the energy to take a bigger feed.
* Continue to help your baby to distinguish between night and day.
* Try to implement the 'pause'. Observe and listen to your baby.
* Establish a bath and bedtime routine, this will help your baby to differentiate between night and day.
* Help your baby to self-settle for naps and at night-time try to put him to bed drowsy but awake. Try to avoid feeding him to sleep.

* Use the same 'sleep cue words' each time you put your baby down for a sleep.

3-6 months

* Some babies may sleep through the night at 3 months and some may still be waking for one or two feeds at night at 6 months. All babies are unique and have different needs, don't compare your baby with your friend's baby.
* If you haven't already implemented a regular bath routine, now is the time to do so.
* If your feeds are close together, increase the intervals between feeds gradually. If your baby is taking a bigger feed he will be more satisfied and will sleep for longer periods.
* Establish a regular daytime pattern of feeding and napping, never feeding just before a sleep.
* Encourage your baby to self-settle, night and day.
* Consider giving the final feed of the day, just before a bath, to disassociate feeding and sleeping.
* DO NOT FEED TO SLEEP – this is key!
* At 6 months, if your baby is still waking for night feeds, you can start to gradually wean him off, if he is healthy and eating well during the day.

Part Four:

SLEEP SOLUTIONS: 6 MONTHS PLUS

19. Have you missed the early boat?

I encourage all parents to establish positive sleep habits early on, however it's never too late to teach your baby to sleep so if you have just picked up this book and your baby is over 6 months old, this part is for you.

If you haven't taught your baby how to settle independently from a young age you need to prepare yourself for a bit of a bumpy ride, which no doubt will involve some crying. Well established sleep habits will take time to change, so consistency is vital.

The crying debate

A cause of great confusion and angst amongst parents is whether it is detrimental to their baby's emotional well-being to allow them to cry. I feel that this is an issue which is often taken out of context and misrepresented in many debates, particularly on the Internet.

My view on crying in general is that allowing your baby to cry is a way of respecting their voice and allowing them to communicate with you. If you quell every cry, you are not responding to your baby's needs as you are not listening to their voice and allowing yourself time to try to interpret their needs.

There are some very strong opinions regarding crying, some that may scare parents into thinking they should

never allow their baby to cry. However, sometimes your baby needs to have a grizzle and a groan to get themselves off to sleep or in between sleep cycles during the night. I advocate simply not responding too quickly when your baby stirs, allow a little time unless you think that there is something wrong or your baby's cry tells you there is.

I absolutely think that you should respond to your baby and that if he is distressed, he is trying to tell you that he has needs which must be met. Pausing and listening does not mean that you are being unresponsive; quite the opposite. Taking time to understand your baby and responding with the appropriate action, whether it's food, touch or warmth is positive parenting and sometimes you may find that having cuddled, rocked and jiggled your baby and found that nothing is calming him, putting him down in his Moses basket or on his play mat is the answer; sometimes babies just need a bit of space and calm as they are over-stimulated.

There are strongly conflicting opinions about sleep training methods which involve leaving your baby to cry for long periods of time and none of these methods should be considered for a baby under 6 months old. There is the school of thought which says that conditioning your baby not to cry by not meeting his needs can result in psychological damage. However, we have other sleep doctors stating that long term sleep deprivation is physically and psychologically damaging and that using a sleep training technique is healthier than continuing this damaging cycle.

I regularly work with families whose babies are sleep deprived and waking between every sleep cycle during the night as they cannot get themselves back to sleep at night without help. This also causes the baby to become fretful during the day and for a sleep deprived parent this is not a healthy situation to be in. The parent may then not be able to make positive parental decisions and may make poor judgements due to their exhaustion. This can have a negative effect on all members of the family. It's a vicious circle, as the more tired a baby is the more difficult he will find it to get to sleep. Therefore teaching your baby to sleep is essential in this situation but should be carried out in a way that meets your baby's needs and offers reassurance.

Leaving your baby to cry for hours on end, day after day or night after night is no doubt damaging but this should not be confused with using a sleep teaching technique where your baby is offered frequent reassurance. Sleep teaching is a short term situation which provides a long term solution and should not be confused with neglecting your baby's needs. Long term sleep deprivation is damaging for the health of you, your baby or child and can have a significant effect on their behaviour and their ability to learn so needs to be addressed for their well-being.

Checklist

Before embarking on any sleep teaching, it is crucial that you have all the building blocks in place, so go through the following checklist first.

Does your baby have a 'sleep association'? What is it?

If your baby is feeding to sleep you need to re-organise your routine so that a feed doesn't come just before sleep. Your baby will find it difficult to fall asleep at first as he doesn't know how to without feeding. You may need to do a lot of soothing, and to begin with you can even go for long walks or take him for a drive to help him to nap. Initially it doesn't matter what you do or how you do it, just focus on not feeding to sleep. The next step will be to move on to one of the settling methods listed below.

Is your baby taking regular daytime naps?

Sleep encourages sleep. In order for your baby to sleep well at night he needs to be well rested. If a baby is overtired his body will produce the hormone cortisol, to help him cope with the fatigue. This gives a 'second wind' effect and makes it harder for your baby to go to sleep and may result in regular night waking and early rising. Work on encouraging good daytime naps. If your baby is taking lots of short naps, gradually space the time between them. Anything less than 45 minutes does not provide your baby with the full physiological benefits that deeper sleep offers so if your baby is having lots of catnaps or short naps, he is not having the benefit of fully restorative sleep. Try to get your baby to have at least one nap a day in his cot, as motion naps do not provide the deep restorative sleep we are aiming for. If your baby is over 6 months old do not let him nap past 3.30–4 p.m.

Do you have a regular, predictable bath routine?

See section 13. This will help your baby to produce the hormone melatonin, which helps regulate sleep/wake cycles. It also provides sleep cues which help the baby to expect sleep. Ensure this is in place before embarking on any sleep training techniques.

Is your baby eating well during the day?

You can't expect your baby to sleep well if he is hungry! Make sure he is taking regular milk feeds during the day with good intervals in between to encourage him to take a bigger and more satisfying feed. If he is over 6 months encourage a good diet so he is not hungry during the night. Certain foods are reported to be sleep inducing, particularly cherries, bananas, warm milk, cottage cheese, yogurt, eggs, chicken, turkey, sweet potatoes, oats and cereals.

Is your baby in good health?

If you have any doubts, seek advice from your GP, health visitor or paediatrician.

20. Sleep teaching techniques

It is unfair to attempt any sleep 'teaching' before the above building blocks are in place. Go through the checklist above before you commence, then:

★ **Choose one of the sleep solution methods below.**

★ **Choose the one which feels most comfortable with you, and stay with it, don't change tack after a few days, you will confuse your baby.**

★ **Ensure that both you and your partner are in agreement. Two teachers are better than one.**

★ **The gentler techniques tend to take longer and need lots of patience but involve less crying.**

★ **Choose a time to start when you can stick to a consistent routine, i.e. not just before you are going on holiday.**

★ **Choose a time when your baby is well and you are well.**

★ **Ensure your baby has a full tummy, ideally having his last feed before your short and soothing bath routine.**

★ **It is crucial that you see it through. Do not make a half-hearted attempt. It's unfair on you and your baby and will make the situation worse.**

Gradual retreat

This is a gentle method whereby you gradually move on to the next degree of separation. Your starting point will be governed by what your baby has become dependent on.

★ **If your baby has always breastfed to sleep, you need to unlatch him when he has stopped vigorously sucking. The easiest way to do this is to gently insert your finger into the corner of his mouth to break the suction and remove your nipple from his mouth. He will probably root and cry as he has previously been allowed to stay sucking on the breast, using it as a pacifier. Try to cuddle and calm him. If you need to allow him to latch on again, do exactly the same thing, when he has finished sucking vigorously, unlatch, calm and cuddle him. Repeat, as necessary. We want him to be sleepy but not asleep.**

* When he has learnt to fall asleep without sucking, you can move on to the next step of settling him in his cot, when he is drowsy. Your baby may find it easier to get to sleep if your partner settles him as he associates mum with food.

* If you have always rocked your baby to sleep in your arms you are ready to move to the next degree of separation. which is laying him in his cot and helping him to settle with your presence.

* After a cuddle, settle your baby into his cot saying 'It's sleep time now' and your reassuring 'sleep cue words'.

* Stay with him, soothe him, gently pat, shush and encourage him to sleep. Sometimes shushing loudly can distract your baby from crying.

* Try to avoid eye contact, do not engage with him. Be boring! However long he cries or tries to fight sleep, the most important thing is that you see this through until sleep is achieved. Stay with him. It may take a long time at first as he will expect to be picked up, especially if he's learnt to fall asleep in your arms, so he needs to understand what you are expecting of him.

* Try not to pick him up and cuddle him, try to give him comfort and reassurance while in his cot. You may need to lean over and almost cuddle him in his cot. However, if he is inconsolable and you really feel

it is necessary, give him a cuddle until he calms and then start the process again making sure he goes back in his cot awake.

★ Your aim is to teach him to go to sleep without your help, so with a gradual retreat process you will move on to the next degree of separation once he has gone to sleep two or three times in this way and when the time taken to achieve sleep has shortened.

★ Do not leave the room until you are sure he is soundly asleep. Wait at least 10 minutes as leaving too early when he may only be partially asleep may disturb him and you may have to start all over again!

★ The next step would be to give less help and intervention, therefore you may give just an occasional pat, shush, or put a reassuring firm hand on his back, again staying with him until he falls asleep.

★ After a couple of successes with this, you may just sit on the floor next to his cot, and once you think he is ready and comfortable falling asleep independently, move completely away once you have settled him.

★ With this method you need to observe, listen and judge when it is time to move on to the next degree of separation, you may even find that your presence is over-stimulating and interferes with your baby going to sleep, in which case, it's time to step back.

* Another starting point that some parents feel comfortable with is laying, with eyes closed, on a camp bed next to their baby's cot. Even though their baby may be crying, they are by their side.

* Whichever starting point you choose, you must keep your goal in mind, which is to give less and less intervention over a period of time and distance yourself until your baby is comfortable to settle alone.

* This is a trust technique and will take time and patience. You are giving the message that you are there for him and will respond when he cries but you do expect him to go to sleep in his cot. By offering him comfort and reassurance, you are modelling the behaviour that a baby or child should follow in terms of how to soothe himself.

* This method will work but you must see it through and be 100 per cent consistent.

* If you allow your baby to cry for half an hour and then give up you are simply teaching him to cry for a fixed period of time.

* Each time he goes to sleep in this way, it will be easier for him the next time.

* Don't try any method two or three times and then give up just as you were about to turn the corner, KEEP GOING!

Pick up and put down

If you do not feel ready for gradual retreat, then this could be the method for you. After following your usual routine, lay your baby in his cot, drowsy but awake, saying your soothing 'sleep words'. If he cries and cannot be calmed, pick him up and comfort him until he is calm and drowsy but not asleep. Put him back in his cot, and repeat this cycle as necessary until he is asleep. This method requires time and patience and for some babies the picking up and putting down may be over-stimulating.

Once your baby has learnt to go to sleep in this way, continue with gradual retreat, as above.

Some parenting advisors suggest that when carrying out this technique you stay with your baby and pick up and cuddle when he is crying but advise you to leave the room as soon as he is quiet. I think this is rewarding the crying and punishing the desired behaviour, I would therefore suggest that with this technique you stay with baby until he is asleep; this will build trust and reassurance.

Controlled crying with reassurance

This method which is sometimes known as 'Check-and-Console' will involve more crying but can work quickly if you are consistent with it. Only use this method with a baby over 6 months old, who is from a safe, secure and loving background.

Timed method

When following this technique, it is important to show your baby that you are being responsive to their needs by returning and providing reassurance, and giving your baby clear and gentle explanations of what you expect of him.

Night one:

* **After a cuddle, settle your baby into his cot saying 'it's sleep time now' and your reassuring 'sleep cue words'.**
* **Leave the room and close the door, either fully or partially, whatever you feel more comfortable with. He will probably cry.**
* **Wait for 2 minutes. Then go back in for 2 minutes and comfort and reassure by laying your hand on him and saying 'shush, shush, there, there, it's sleep time now'. Don't engage and avoid eye contact.**
* **Leave the room for 3 minutes and then go back in for 2 minutes. Building up to 5 minutes out of the room on the first night. Keep repeating this process until he is asleep, however long it takes!**
* **If your older baby is standing against the side of his cot, gently lay him down.**

Night two:

★ **Start with 5 minutes out of the room and up to 2 minutes in, building up to 7 minutes out of the room.**

Night three:

★ **Start with 7 minutes out of the room and 1 minute in, building up to 10 minutes out of the room.**
★ **Repeat night three timings for subsequent nights, if necessary.**

The most important thing is to listen to his cries. If he is grizzling or the volume of his cry is reducing, do not go back to him, or you may disturb his self-settling process. Only go back and reassure if you think his crying is escalating into distress.

If you prefer not to watch the clock, you can follow the same process but returning to reassure your baby at more randomly spaced intervals depending on the sound of his cries, especially if you find that your reassurances are antagonising him more.

If he becomes overly distressed, you may need to pick him up and calm him, but do not allow him to fall asleep in your arms. When he is calm put him back in the cot and start again.

This is a learning process, he may cry and shout with anger and frustration as he is not sure what is expected of him – he's never done it before! You are teaching him that you expect him to go to sleep in his cot while giving him regular reassurances so he does not feel abandoned. He will get the message if you are consistent. Try to interpret his cries, and assess when you need to go in and reassure.

Cry it out

Most parents I come across are uncomfortable with this method, so it is not a technique that I would recommend in this book but I will explain it, as it's described in many books and websites and some think that it is the quickest and simplest method. It is basically as it sounds, you leave your baby to cry for as long as it takes them to get to sleep without doing any checking and consoling. The theory behind it is that your baby quickly learns that his cries won't be rewarded with your presence. This technique attracts the most controversy.

Key points to remember:

★ **Give yourself small, realistic goals.**
★ **Whichever method you choose, it is essential that you see it through until sleep is achieved. These methods do work if you are 100 per cent consistent. Do not give up after two or three tries. Your baby will be confused.**

★ Prepare yourself – this will be exceptionally hard. No-one likes to hear their baby cry but you will be giving regular reassurances. Remind yourself why you are teaching your baby to sleep; sleep deprivation is damaging to your baby and the whole family.

★ With any change in routine, things can get worse before they get better.

★ Quite often, following a successful period, you may have a test night or two of regression. Be persistent and consistent and you should get back on track.

★ You need to send a clear message to your baby or toddler about what is expected, so whatever is happening at one sleep situation, needs to happen for all sleep situations; night-time, nap times and if your baby or toddler wakes during the night.

★ Keep a sleep diary detailing what you do and how long it takes your baby to get to sleep. You should start to see improvements after 3 or 4 days. However, the older your baby is the longer it may take, so do not give up, that would be unfair on your baby and make it doubly hard if you re-attempt at another time.

★ Real change for regular improved nights and naps may take one week or may take three or four, depending on the method you choose and how quickly you progress with it. Putting the effort in now will pay dividends in the future.

★ Always put your baby down for sleeps before he gets overtired, he will find it easier to settle. Look for sleep signs and keep a sleep diary to help you understand your baby's rhythms.

★ If your baby becomes unwell at all during this period of teaching, give him the comfort he needs and then go back to it when he is well again.

★ A baby's needs and sleep routine will change over time, so look for the signs of this and adapt your routine, as necessary.

★ If you have a bad day, put it behind you and move on. We all have bad days.

★ Be positive! Don't dread putting your baby down for his sleep. He will sense your anxiety. Put him down to sleep in a positive way and fully expect him to sleep. When he learns to settle himself he will love going to sleep!

Consistency is key!

At 6 months old, James was waking two or three times a night and I nursed him back to sleep. With Stephanie's help I taught him to self-settle. I used the controlled crying with reassurance technique. It was incredibly hard to hear him cry but in just 3 days he had learnt to self-settle, his sleeping had improved and after 10 days he was sleeping through the night. 99

Miriam, mother of James, 7 months old.

21. Baby sleep: solutions to common problems

My baby will only fall asleep on the breast or while bottle feeding...

Babies are not born with sleep associations, and unfortunately, falling asleep during a feed is a sleep association that you've taught your baby. You need to teach your baby to self-settle. If you always feed your baby to sleep this is the only way he will be able to go to sleep. In the first 6–8 weeks, don't worry too much, this is a time for getting to know your baby, establishing feeding and bonding. Your baby is small and sleepy so sometimes falling asleep while feeding can't be avoided. However, even at this age try to occasionally put baby down to sleep, drowsy but awake.

If your baby is older, avoid feeding just before your baby is due a sleep. You need to completely disassociate feeding and sleeping. A good daytime sleep/awake pattern to follow is: sleep, feed, play, repeat. Furthermore, this will encourage your baby to take a good, full feed as he won't be falling asleep while feeding. Refer to section 13 – Routine/feeding and napping.

If you are breastfeeding, your baby is likely to be using the nipple as a pacifier. This is a habit that many mothers find the most difficult to break. The first step is to start to unlatch your baby from the breast when he has finished vigorously sucking. If he roots for the nipple again, then try to cuddle and soothe him. If he continues to root and cry, you can let him suck again if necessary but repeat the same process, taking him off the breast as soon as he has finished sucking vigorously. Continue this process every time you feed. It's essential to differentiate between feeding and nursing for comfort, otherwise your baby is going to need your help to resettle many times during the night.

I would suggest using a gradual retreat process to help your baby to settle without feeding. See section 20 – Sleep teaching techniques.

Our baby will only fall asleep in our bed...
This is because you have taught your baby to fall asleep in this way. The earlier you teach your baby to self-settle in his own cot or Moses basket, the easier it will be. He won't like it to begin with. This is because every time you

have tried before, he's cried, you've given up and taken him into your bed. Of course he will cry as this is what you have taught him. So, choose a settling technique (see sections 15 and 20) and prepare to see it through however long it takes. You will be amazed how quickly your baby will learn if you do the same thing every time. Time, repetition and consistency are key.

> *Charlotte had never slept well and at 5 months old I could only get her to sleep in our bed at night and in my arms during the day. I was exhausted. Every time I put Charlotte in her cot she screamed but, in picking her up the whole time, I was inadvertently rewarding her cries and I didn't know what else to do. Stephanie taught me to soothe Charlotte in her cot, and she did scream for 35 minutes on the first day, but I stayed with her until sleep was achieved. This was the secret, to see it through, as every day the time got shorter and shorter. Within a week Charlotte was sleeping in her cot during the day and the following week during the night.*

I was determined not to make the same mistakes with our second baby and I started to teach her to self-settle from week one! She is a great sleeper. I just put her down in her cot, and she goes to sleep. No props, just a soft, cloth comforter.

Angela, mother of Charlotte and Savanna, now aged 4 years and 1 year.

My baby won't settle...

Choose a settling technique that you are comfortable with and suits your parenting style. If you are consistent and do the same thing every time, your baby will learn to settle, if you try a new technique for only three times and then give up, you are sure to fail. Your baby will become confused as he has not had sufficient opportunity to learn a new behaviour, and you will reinforce the crying. Time, repetition and consistency are key, otherwise you may give up just as your baby was starting to get the message and succeed.

It took me 40 minutes to settle my baby in his cot for a nap and then he only slept for half an hour...

Once your baby has mastered the art of self-settling his naps will become longer and longer. Consistency **will** pay off. If it's been difficult one day, don't try again on the same day, give yourself and your baby a break and take him out for a long walk, or a drive instead. Tomorrow is a new day, be positive and continue with your teaching process.

My 6-month-old baby is waking every 2–3 hours in the night...

This behaviour is usually due to your baby not settling independently at the start of the night. Babies rouse between sleep cycles and if you've taught your baby to go to sleep with an inappropriate sleep association or prop he will struggle to connect his sleep cycles independently during these partial wakings. The most common sleep associations are feeding or rocking to sleep. Whatever it is, your baby will be dependent on it throughout the night. It is essential to teach your baby to self-settle with no props or inappropriate associations. See section 7 – Sleep associations.

My baby will only catnap...

If your baby is self-settling this should improve as he becomes more proficient at connecting his sleep cycles. From around 6 months old you are aiming for two to three naps during the day with the longest one being at lunchtime so if this continues to be short, take a look at your routine and timings. An ideal routine at around 6–9 months would be a 45–60 minute nap in the morning, 1.5

hours around lunchtime and a short nap before tea time so your baby is not overtired at bath time.

If the situation doesn't improve, but if your baby sleeps well in the pushchair you could try taking him for a long walk in the middle of the day with the aim of getting him to sleep for two sleep cycles (1.5 hours). Do this for four or five days. The aim of this will be to get his body used to sleeping for the longer period. Then return to midday cot naps and hopefully he will find it easier to connect his sleep cycles.

Another trick is to wait outside his room at around the time he usually wakes. As soon as he stirs, go in and do anything that will help him get back to sleep. Rub his tummy, shush, pat. This is a time to ignore the usual rules and help him to resettle. Repeat as necessary, to help him achieve at least 45 minutes of sleep. If you do this for a week or so, you should find that your baby starts to sleep longer.

My 8-month-old baby is waking at 5 a.m. and then having a 2 hour early morning nap...
This long early morning nap is perpetuating the early rising. Gradually move the morning nap forwards in 15 minute increments until you reach 9 a.m. and gradually shorten the length of it to no longer than one hour. Aim for your baby's long nap to be at lunchtime.

My 4-month-old baby is feeding every 2 hours...
If there is no medical reason why your baby should feed so regularly, gradually increase the time between feeds. For the first couple of days feed every 2.25 hours, for the second couple of days feed every 2.5 hours and so on until you are feeding every 3–4 hours. You will need to keep your baby occupied and distracted to elongate the time between feeds. Over time he should start to take a bigger feed and this will satisfy him for longer periods between feeds.

My daughter is 6.5 months old and I would really like to establish a regular routine for her. Can you help?
A typical routine at this age would be as follows, but remember all babies are unique so keep a sleep diary and try to adapt a routine which suits your baby's rhythms and fits in with your lifestyle.

7.00 a.m.: Awake. Breast or bottle feed followed by breakfast.

9.00–9.30: Nap – one sleep cycle – 45–60 minutes. Breast or bottle on waking, if needed.

11.30–12.00: Lunch.

12.00–12.30: Long nap – two sleep cycles – 1.5–2 hours.

2.30–3.00: Breast or bottle feed.

4.00–4.30: Short nap (depending on earlier naps). Babies don't usually settle well in their cots for this late afternoon nap, so maybe go for a walk. We don't want her to be too tired at bedtime or she will fall asleep during her pre-bath feed.

5.00: Tea.

6.15: Breast or bottle.

6.30: Bath.

7.00: Sleep.

I give my baby a dream feed at 10 p.m. but he still wakes 2 hours later...

I would suggest that you stop dream feeding and allow your baby to regulate his own body clock. During the first part of the night your baby is most likely to be in a deep sleep and I don't think it's fair to stimulate his digestive system when he is not hungry. You may find that he sleeps for a much longer stretch without the dream feed. See section 12 – Dream feeds.

My baby keeps losing her dummy in the night...

People often ask me my thoughts on dummies and if it works for you and your baby then it's fine, but if it's causing a problem and contributing to night-time waking, you either need to consider weaning your baby off it, or if he is old enough to replace it himself, put extra dummies in his cot so they will be easier to find. Alternatively, you can purchase safe dummy clips which attach the dummy to the baby's clothes or you can buy soft cloth toys with Velcro hands to attach the dummies to, making them easier for small hands to find in the night.

My baby has started to stand up in her cot...
This can be a particular problem when your baby does not know how to lower herself. Practise during the daytime by playing pulling up and lowering back down games. It can be most frustrating when you lower your baby at night and she stands straight back up again but be careful not to turn this into a game!

My baby is 8 months old and still waking for a night feed...
If your baby is in good health and eating well during the day, you can wean him off this feed. If he is breastfed, gradually reduce the amount of minutes you offer him each night. When he has got used to taking a very small amount, stop offering milk and use one of the settling techniques. See section 20 – Sleep teaching techniques.

If your baby is bottle fed, reduce the volume of milk you give him gradually over a number of nights. Once your baby is used to taking a smaller amount, stop offering a bottle and use one of the settling techniques. Some parenting advisors recommend adding less and less milk powder to the bottle making it less satisfying and calorific. This technique can work, however, you may find that your baby still wakes to suck for comfort.

My 5-month-old son has been sleeping through until 4 a.m. for the past month and has recently started waking at 12.30 a.m. Should I feed him then?

Don't automatically assume that your son needs a feed at that time. Try to settle him back to sleep without feeding, if he is genuinely hungry he will not settle and will be sure to let you know. In which case, he may be going through a growth spurt.

My 9-month-old twins are rocked to sleep in their bouncy chairs and then we lift them into their cots but they are repeatedly waking in the night and are difficult to resettle...

Your babies need to learn to settle to sleep in their cots. When they rouse between sleep cycles in the night, they are finding themselves in a different place to where they fell asleep and do not know how they got there. This is making them feel insecure and they do not know how to get themselves back to sleep without being rocked.

Part Five:
CASE STUDIES

Willow - 16 weeks old

Situation - Willow's parents contacted me as Willow was waking repeatedly during the night, literally every hour. Both parents were exhausted and hadn't achieved more than 3 hours total sleep at night for the previous few weeks. Each time Willow woke at night she was fed or rocked back to sleep. During the evening she slept in mum or dad's arms until they went to bed and then she was put into her cot when she was soundly sleeping. During the day she was fed or rocked to sleep in her bouncy chair. The night before I met the family, Willow had woken eight times between midnight and 5 a.m. and had then slept in the parents' bed through their desperation to get a little more sleep!

Diagnosis - Willow had never fallen asleep independently, this resulted in her waking every time she roused during the night and needing to be fed or rocked back to sleep again. She also had no night-time routine to help her to differentiate night and day. In the early hours her waking was rewarded by coming into her parents' bed.

Solution - I advised Willow's parents to establish a short predictable bath routine, commencing around 6.30 p.m., feeding Willow before her bath and then helping her to self-settle in her cot by using a gradual retreat process.

During the day, the parents were asked to help Willow to settle in any way that didn't involve the feeding-to-sleep association. Initially, this might be going for a walk or rocking, and once night times had improved they could work on settling her into her cot in the daytime.

Outcome – As Willow had never gone to sleep in her cot before, she needed a lot of soothing and comfort to begin with. On the first night she, of course, cried as she didn't know what was expected of her, but I had explained to the parents the importance of this teaching process and how it was crucial to see it through until sleep was achieved. Mum said that she was almost cuddling Willow in her cot while stroking her head gently and saying reassuring gentle words. Mum used long and short shushing sounds and when Willow was really worked up she gently rolled her on her side and patted her back until the crying had subsided. This proved effective for Willow. In these early days you do whatever is necessary to soothe to sleep but try to avoid lifting unless you really have to.

On the first night Willow took 49 minutes to get to sleep and cried most of the time, however, mum stayed by her side for the whole time and consoled and reassured her. On this very first night she only woke once at 2.15 a.m. and had a breastfeed, settled back to sleep and then woke again at 3.20 a.m. when Mum was able to soothe her back to sleep without lifting her. She woke for the day at 6.30 a.m. An amazing first night!

On night two, Willow took 31 minutes to get to sleep and on night three, 24 minutes. As time went on Willow took less and less time to get to sleep, and mum and dad used less interaction and soothing and worked on gradually retreating to the next degree of separation.

From the very start of the new routine Willow only woke once or twice during the night. She was at the perfect age to 'sleep teach'. She did start waking early in the morning but instead of bringing her into their bed which would reward and reinforce the waking, her parents soothed her and gave her comfort in her cot.

Willow's parents were also less quick to respond to her in the night when she stirred and grizzled as they understood that in order for her to learn to connect her sleep cycles they had to give her the opportunity to do so. They had previously been picking her up every time she cried, probably waking her unnecessarily.

Once the night-time sleeping had improved they focused their attention on getting a daytime feeding and napping routine in place and worked on Willow having at least one nap a day in her cot.

Although it's difficult for any parent to hear their baby cry, Willow proved that by allowing some crying during this teaching process prevented long term regular waking and crying which may have resulted in severe sleep deprivation that is unhealthy to both baby and parents.

Mum's comments:
'One of the most valuable things you have taught me is simply to "allow Willow her voice". Before you said that to me, I was always desperate to find the quickest way to stop her from crying. Now I understand that sometimes she just needs to cry and I've learnt to differentiate her cries much better.

'You have literally transformed our lives so we can all sleep again! I can now put Willow down to sleep in the evening, stand back (out of her eyeline) and watch her grizzle and groan for 10 minutes and then fall asleep. I know she is ready for me to put her down and leave the room, but I think this will be harder for me than her as I rather like this bit of the day, watching my baby fall asleep!'

Tamara – 12 months old

Situation – Early rising. Tamara had learnt to self-settle and generally went to bed at about 7 p.m. but woke at 5 a.m., just a little too early to start the day. Mum and dad had tried feeding her and putting her back to bed but she would not settle so they started the day. However, this meant that Tamara was tired again by 7 a.m. and would go back down for a 1.5-2 hour nap. She would then have another shorter nap around lunchtime and would still be tired in the evening. Her parents had also tried putting her to bed later in the hope that she would wake later, but this was unsuccessful.

Diagnosis – Typical sleep requirements at this age are approximately 11 hours at night (but 12, if you are lucky) and 2-2.5 hours during the day. The longer nap should be around lunchtime but should not go past 3.30 p.m. Early rising is very common and often the most difficult situation to deal with as your baby has had a good chunk of sleep and is feeling revitalised even if you are not! Early rising is usually perpetuated by the following: rewarding the waking, learnt hunger or wrongly scheduled naps. In Tamara's case all three of these were happening. Tamara was allowed to start the day at 5 a.m. and enjoyed the attention given to her at this time. She also had a feed then, so had learnt to be hungry at that time and she was napping too early, thereby the first nap of the day was really a part of the night-time sleep that had become disjointed from the rest of the night. She was also overtired by the time she went to bed in the evening, which causes the body to produce the hormone cortisol, which can perpetuate early rising.

Solution – The parents were advised firstly to ensure a regular predictable night-time bed/bath routine. The morning nap needed to be shifted forwards and shortened as this was allowing Tamara to compensate for the lack of night-time sleep. If it was shifted forward too quickly Tamara would get overtired so her parents were advised to move this nap forward slowly in 15 minute increments until they reached 9 a.m. and to gradually shorten this nap to a maximum of one hour. The morning feed was also moved forward in 15 minute increments until Tamara's first feed of the day was at 6.30 a.m. When Tamara woke early her parents were advised to leave her to play/cry in her cot until the agreed time each day.

Outcome – On day one, Tamara woke at 5 a.m. as usual. She was left for 15 minutes in which time she did cry but was not overly distressed. The following day her parents did not go to her until 5.15 once again and the subsequent two days she was left until 5.30 and so on. Every two days the time before her parents entered her room extended by 15 minutes. During this time her morning nap was also shifted forward slowly and although she was tired she was not left to get overtired. She was not happy about being left to her own devices in the mornings but she had some soft toys in her cot and soon learnt that her waking wouldn't be rewarded.

Her wake up time gradually moved forwards but it took about 4 weeks before her wake up time adjusted to 6–6.30 a.m. With some babies it may take a week and for others it may take a month but if you are consistent the situation will improve.

Another point to consider if you have an early riser is that your baby's bedtime may be too late! I know this sounds crazy but it's true, if a baby goes to bed with high cortisol levels because he is overtired, he will find it more difficult to go to sleep, may be unsettled during the night and is more likely to wake early. Slowly bring his bedtime forwards.

Another common reason for early rising is that the parents bring the baby/child into their bed in order to get some more precious sleep themselves. When you are exhausted you will do anything for a little more sleep but this totally rewards and reinforces the behaviour. Of course your baby will wake early for this special treat and the waking time will probably get earlier and earlier. You have to work through this so you all can benefit from a full night's sleep. Make a plan and be consistent!

Mum's comments:

'Stephanie explained to us from the start that early rising is one of the most common situations and one of the trickiest to resolve. However, I'm so pleased we worked through it, as starting the day at 5 a.m. was starting to take its toll! Alongside that, I am going back to work shortly and Tamara's early rising and subsequent long morning nap just would not fit in with daycare.'

Oliver - 11 months old

Situation – Repeated night waking, unsettled in the early evening and very little daytime sleep.

Oliver's parents had followed 'attachment parenting' with Oliver as he was very unsettled as a young baby. He co-slept at night and during the day they carried him in a sling where he would have his daytime naps. This had worked quite well when he was younger but at 11 months old he was a big boy and was too heavy to carry in a sling for long periods. He therefore had daytime naps in his pushchair or in the car as he had never slept in a cot. At night his mum would breastfeed him to sleep and he would settle in the parental bed but would wake up repeatedly until his parents came to bed and he would wake regularly during the night to feed. He was often overtired during the day and his parents were exhausted too as a result of continually disturbed sleep.

As a sleep consultant, I always follow the parents' wishes and offer solutions that the parents feel comfortable with. In Oliver's case, the parents were clear from the start that they did not want to consider 'controlled crying' or similar and that they ideally wanted to continue to co-sleep.

Diagnosis – When a baby rouses during the night in between sleep cycles, they need to find themselves in exactly the same situation as they fell asleep in. They will then feel safe and able to connect to their next sleep cycle. In Oliver's case he was falling asleep while nursing, lying down with mum and sometimes with dad as well. When he was asleep they would creep downstairs, he would miss their presence when he roused and subsequently wake up again. During the night he needed mum to nurse him back to sleep between sleep cycles as he had never learnt to connect his sleep cycles independently. The regular night feeds were sometimes causing him to open his bowels in the night and also affecting his daytime appetite. At his age, Oliver did not require night feeds for nourishment as he had a good diet during the day. Daytime sleep was a particular issue as Oliver needed to learn to sleep in a cot in order to achieve good physiologically restorative sleep in a safe environment.

Solution – We had no plans for a quick fix solution with Oliver, just a gentle step by step approach. Our first aim was to disassociate feeding and sleeping so during the first week the parents were asked to follow a regular bath routine with Oliver. Then mum breastfed him in a chair but didn't allow him to fall asleep while nursing. Then mum or dad would lay with Oliver in the parental bed, soothing him as necessary until he was asleep. If he woke before the parents came to bed, mum or dad would lay with him again and soothe or cuddle him without feeding. After the first week mum and dad were asked to give less and less intervention to help Oliver get to sleep, so instead of cuddling to sleep, they were to just lay by his side without giving eye contact or interacting with him, and then after a few days lay with their backs to him and then gradually move to the edge of the bed, eventually just sitting on the side of the bed. I also asked for just one parent to be with him as they had both previously been present when he went to sleep.

Once Oliver had learnt to go to sleep without nursing we needed to teach him to sleep in his cot as it was essential for him to achieve good daytime naps so he was not overtired at night. Oliver's most predictable daytime sleep was his morning nap around 10 a.m. We decided on a gradual retreat approach where mum would settle him into his cot, sit on the floor at eyelevel (to encourage him to stay laying down rather than stand against the side of the cot) and to pat, soothe and make gentle shushing sounds. This obviously would involve crying as Oliver had never slept in a cot before so didn't know what was expected of him. I expected Oliver to resist sleeping, but reassured mum that because she was staying with him at all times he would not feel abandoned as she was there to give him love and comfort and she had a secure and strong attachment with him. For his health and well-being it was essential for him to learn the skill of self-settling in the safety of a cot. Mum was advised that she must see this process through until sleep was achieved and not give up otherwise she would be teaching him to cry for a fixed time. I advised that each time he fell asleep in this way, he would find it easier the next time. Every few days, mum was to give less and less intervention with helping Oliver to sleep until she was eventually just sitting by his side and then she was to gradually move her chair away from the cot.

The next step was to reduce night-time feeds by cutting out feeds at particular times.

Outcome – Oliver responded very positively to not feeding to sleep as he still had mum and/or dad to lay down with him to begin with so it was a very gradual withdrawal process. They slowly gave less and less intervention to help him get to sleep and this quickly resulted in him not waking during the early evening period, when he was in his deep sleep phase.

Teaching him to sleep in a cot took a period of only five days. As expected, on day one, he stood up and cried a lot but his mum stayed by his side and kept encouraging him to lay down and sleep, while soothing him. It took one hour on the first day and then he slept soundly for 40 minutes. On day two, it took 35 minutes and he slept for 45 minutes. On day three, his cries changed to protests and it took 55 minutes. Day four, 30 minutes, again protesting, but not crying. On day five, it took only 5 minutes with no crying! Over time his naps became longer and he enjoyed going to sleep in his cot. Mum tended to stay with him until he went to sleep as this was her preference.

Oliver learnt very quickly to sleep in his cot and both myself and his parents were very pleased with his response. I think that this type of trust technique of staying with him suited the parenting style he was used to and he was also of an age where he understood what mum was asking of him.

Interestingly, once he learnt to nap in his cot, when he was put in the parental bed in the evenings, he pointed to his cot. His parents felt that this was his way of telling them he was ready for his own space, so he would start the evening in his cot and possibly end up in their bed if he fed in the night. Although this arrangement is unusual it was an excellent compromise for all. He was sleeping well in the daytime, settling in his own cot in the evenings, so mum and dad could have an evening to themselves and he naturally started to wake less during the night for feeds as he was able to self-settle. It was a gradual gentle process which resulted in the whole family achieving better quality sleep.

Mum's comments:
'Teaching Oliver to sleep in his cot has transformed our lives. My parents sometimes look after him when I am working and this now means that he can have his daytime naps at their house. He has also happily slept in a travel cot while we were on holiday. In the early hours we still sometimes co-sleep too. Stephanie worked with us to provide a solution that suited us and our style of parenting and we are all now enjoying more sleep!'

Part Six

FURTHER RESOURCES AND INFORMATION

22. Sleep diary

Use your sleep diary to help you understand your baby's sleep patterns, and then try to regulate your daily feeding and napping routine.

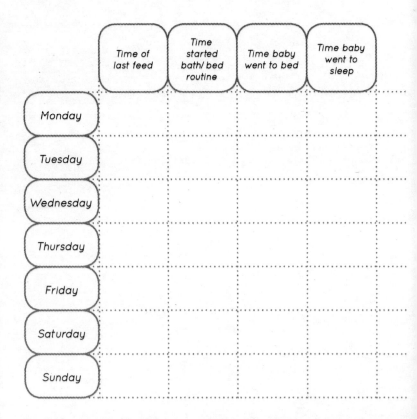

	Time of last feed	Time started bath/ bed routine	Time baby went to bed	Time baby went to sleep
Monday				
Tuesday				
Wednesday				
Thursday				
Friday				
Saturday				
Sunday				

If your baby sleeps around the same time each day, he will find it easier to fall asleep. Try to avoid feeding just before a nap, as this will create a sleep association.

'Additional Information' can include notes about outings, health, what worked well with regard to settling your baby, etc.

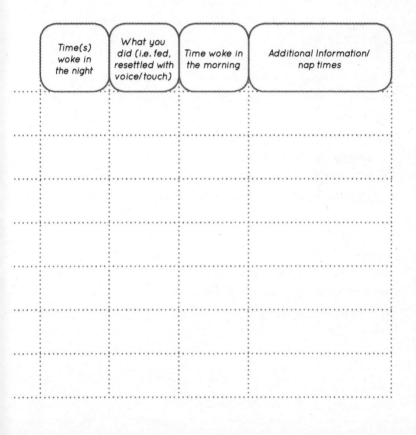

Time(s) woke in the night	What you did (i.e. fed, resettled with voice/touch)	Time woke in the morning	Additional Information/ nap times

23. Top sleep tips

When your baby is 3-6 months old, you can strongly influence when sleep occurs as babies respond well to routine and can differentiate between night and day. This is your window of opportunity to establish good sleep habits.

Here are my top sleep tips. Keep them in a handy place, such as on the fridge door or at the front of your diary to refer to:

1. Babies need to learn to fall asleep alone without any external props or associations. Props come in many forms and may include feeding to sleep by breast or bottle, rocking, cuddling, patting, music or a dummy. If your baby is reliant on one or more of these to fall asleep, they will need it each time they wake in between sleep cycles, which can be several times a night.

2. Going to sleep is learnt behaviour. Encouraging your baby to learn to fall asleep independently is one of the most helpful things you can do to prevent or resolve settling and waking problems. Use a gradual retreat process if necessary.

3. At the start of the night, try to keep your baby awake while feeding and place him in his cot when he is drowsy but not asleep.

4. If your baby wakes during the night give him the opportunity to settle himself. Pause, listen and observe.

5. If you need to feed him during the night, have minimal interaction, only change his nappy if necessary and place him back in his cot straight after his feed, soothing as necessary.

6. Try to establish a positive sleep association i.e. give your baby a safe, special soft toy or a soft cloth so this can become something he associates with sleep and it gives him comfort. Choose something that is replaceable.

7. Establish a regular bedtime. This will regulate your baby's body clock and ensure healthy sleep/wake patterns. Aim for an early bedtime so your baby does not become overtired.

8. Create a predictable bedtime routine lasting no longer than 30–45 minutes. This might include quiet time, bath, pyjamas, feed, then maybe a short quiet story to make a break between feeding and sleeping to avoid creating an association. Alternatively, from around 4 months, consider giving the last feed before the bath.

9. Try to keep daytime naps and feeds regular and consistent. Again, do not feed to sleep. Try to time

your feeds so that they are not just before a nap. Good daytime naps help good night-time sleeping so don't let anyone tell you that exhausting your baby and missing daytime naps will help them to sleep better at night. Just don't allow the last daytime nap to be too late and interfere with bedtime.

10. Let your baby have a voice! Don't try to quell every cry. This is the only way for your baby to communicate with you, so in order for you to understand his needs, pause and listen and try to learn to differentiate between his cries. Babies often grizzle themselves to sleep, this is normal.

11. If you are breastfeeding, try to avoid drinking caffeine especially at the end of the day and you may want to consider introducing an occasional bottle early enough to prevent later rejection. There are a number of breast-feeding friendly bottles and teats available which emulate the breast feeding process.

12. If your baby is still having night feeds at 6 months and is healthy and feeding well during the day, you can now begin to wean him off these night feeds.

13. Be consistent! Whatever is happening at one sleep situation needs to be happening at all sleep situations to send a clear message about what is expected. This includes when your baby wakes during the night. If you occasionally take your baby into bed with you to sleep but expect him to sleep in his cot at other times he will become confused.

Remember, if you are making changes it takes **TIME**, **REPETITION** and **CONSISTENCY**.

24. Useful organisations

The Lullaby Trust – www.lullabytrust.org.uk

National Childbirth Trust – www.nct.org.uk

Baby Centre – www.babycentre.co.uk

The Twins and Multiple Births Association –
www.tamba.org.uk

Homestart – www.home-start.org.uk

For information on breastfeeding-friendly bottles –
www.medela.com
www.habermanbaby.com
www.playtexbaby.com

THE NEW PARENTS' SURVIVAL GUIDE

The first three months

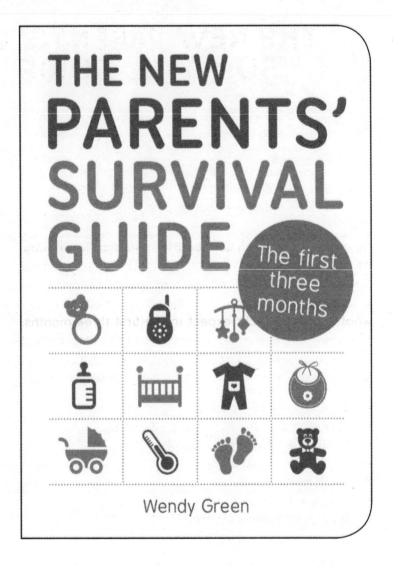

Wendy Green